THE KIDS BOOK OF THE NIGHT SKY

BY ANN LOVE & JANE DRAKE

ILLUSTRATED BY HEATHER COLLINS

KIDS CAN PRESS

ACKNOWLEDGMENTS

The authors wish to acknowledge the contribution to this book of the following people: Henry Barnett; Vic Barnett; Andrew Bell; George Court; Charlie Drake; Jim, Steph, Brian and Madeline Drake; Maddy Ewins; Ted Larkin; Jeff and Rob Lewis; David, Melanie, Jennifer and Adrian Love; Luke and Olivia Love Racine; Andy Nardone; Mark Salmoni; Ben Silcox and Jack Spitler.

We greatly appreciate the thoughtful and expert advice of Dr. Wayne Cannon, Dr. Paul Delaney and Dr. Ian McGregor.

We would like to thank Terence Dickinson, whose publications have fuelled our lifelong fascination with the night sky.

We marvel at the steady orbit of our editor, Laurie Wark, who guided this book toward Earth for several years.

And, finally, thanks to Valerie Hussey and the exceptional earthlings who work at Kids Can Press.

Kids Can Press is a /o∩us™ Entertainment company

Text © 2004 Ann Love and Jane Drake
Illustrations © 2004 Heather Collins

Kids Can Press acknowledges the financial support of the Government of Ontario, through the Ontario Media Development Corporation's Ontario Book Initiative; the Ontario Arts Council; the Canada Council for the Arts; and the Government of Canada, through the BPIDP, for our publishing activity

Published in Canada by
Kids Can Press Ltd.
29 Birch Avenue
Toronto, ON M4V 1E2

Published in the U.S. by
Kids Can Press Ltd.
2250 Military Road
Tonawanda, NY 14150

www.kidscanpress.com

Edited by Laurie Wark
Designed by Karen Powers
Printed in China by WKT Company Limited

The hardcover edition of this book is smyth sewn casebound.
The paperback edition of this book is limp sewn with a drawn-on cover.

CM 04 0 9 8 7 6 5 4 3 2 1
CM PA 04 0 9 8 7 6 5 4 3 2 1

National Library of Canada Cataloguing in Publication Data

Love, Ann
    The kids book of the night sky / written by Ann Love and Jane Drake ; illustrated by Heather Collins.

Includes index.

ISBN 1-55337-357-X (bound). ISBN 1-55337-128-3 (pbk.)

1. Astronomy — Juvenile literature. I. Drake, Jane II. Collins, Heather III. Title.

QB46.L69 2004   j520   C2003-904815-2

*This book is dedicated to family, friends and
starlit nights past, present and yet to come*

CONTENTS

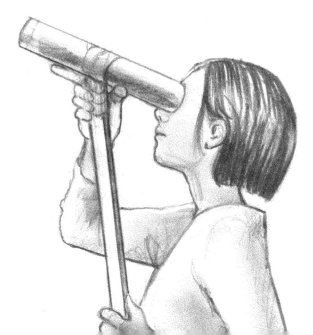

COUNTDOWN TO NIGHTTIME

Thousands of years ago, kids knew the night sky well. They connected the stars into the shapes and stories of people, animals and monsters. Using the stars, they could tell the time and find their way home for supper.

If you live north of the equator, in the Northern Hemisphere, this book will help you sharpen your star sense. Take it skywatching from dusk to dawn, season to season, and you'll learn to tell the date, time and direction from the stars. Find out how to spot dozens of constellations, and then read the amazing stories of the heroes, villains and creatures featured in them.

You'll need to prepare for the night's all-star show before the Sun goes down. In this section, follow the tips to pick the best outdoor seating for your night sky viewing. Compare an ancient story and modern scientific theories about our own daytime star, the Sun. Make a handy four-season planisphere to track the nighttime stars and constellations. And don't forget to craft an astronomer's log so you can record your remarkable sightings.

CITY LIGHTS, COUNTRY NIGHTS

There's free admission to the longest-running show in the Universe, "The Night Sky," now in its 14 billionth year. To get the best view, take a few moments to prepare before dark.

CHOOSE THE SITE

- Have an adult help you choose a site where you have a clear view of the sky. A flat, open area such as a deck, lawn, field or patio is best.

- Avoid trees, water or uneven, rough ground.

- Set out lawn chairs, air mattresses, ground sheets, sleeping bags or blankets

- If you have a telescope, set it up ahead of time, making sure it's on stable ground. Telescopes work best when they're the same temperature as the air.

PLAN YOUR OUTFIT

- Wear dark-colored clothing that is appropriate for the weather and insect repellant.

- Take a hooded sweatshirt for warmth.

- Wear shoes to avoid stubbing your toes in the dark.

PREPARE YOUR SIGHT

- Turn off all the lights inside and out. In about twenty minutes, your eyes will adapt and your pupils will dilate, or open fully. Keep your best night vision by avoiding looking at any light source other than in the sky. One glimpse of light, and your eyes will need another twenty minutes to adjust.

KNOW NORTH

You'll navigate the sky with ease once you can use the Big Dipper to find the North Star.

- Look for a group of seven bright stars shaped like a soup ladle with a crooked handle — you've found the Big Dipper.

- The two stars at the front of the ladle are called the pointer stars.

- Draw an imaginary line from the bottom of the ladle through the pointer stars and you'll end up at Polaris, the North Star.

DARK IS AN ENDANGERED SPACE!

You've heard of air and water pollution, but did you know there's light pollution, too? Viewed from outer space, Earth gives off a twenty-four-hour glow from streetlights, signs and buildings — much of it wasted light that shines all night long while people sleep. Light bounces off the dust and smog that hover over cities, making the sky bright enough to outshine many stars. Telescopes have difficulty working in this light, and some astronomical observatories are being shut down because the sky is too bright. So turn off your lights to save electricity and see more stars.

THE SUN IS A STAR

The Sun is only 150 million km (93 million mi.) from Earth. That may sound far away, but compared to Alpha Centauri — our next closest star — the Sun is very close. Sunlight takes just over eight minutes to reach us, but light from Alpha Centauri takes more than four years to reach Earth.

Because the Sun is so close, we think we know everything about it. But what do we know? Take this quiz to find out. Figure out the answers by reading the information on the next page (or check the answer box on page 144).

1. The Sun is bigger and brighter than most other stars.

☐ True or ☐ false?

2. The surface of the Sun is clear and spotless.

☐ True or ☐ false?

3. The surface of the Sun is calm.

☐ True or ☐ false?

4. Particles from the Sun never reach Earth.

☐ True or ☐ false?

5. The Sun circles Earth once a day, traveling from east to west across the sky.

☐ True or ☐ false?

6. In the daytime, the Sun is the only star in the sky.

☐ True or ☐ false?

- The Sun is a middle-aged star of medium size and brightness.

- Dark patches called sunspots can appear on the Sun. They are cool compared to the rest of the Sun's surface. Sunspots are areas of intense magnetism and usually last only a few days.

- The Sun's surface is covered with gas bubbles called granules, some the size of a continent on Earth. New granules constantly boil up to the surface, last about five minutes, then sink below the surface.

- The upper atmosphere of the Sun, or corona, blows a steady stream of particles into space. This solar wind takes several days to reach Earth.

- The Sun moves through the universe with all the other stars but does not circle Earth. Earth and the other planets orbit the Sun. Earth spins on its axis once every twenty-four hours, but since we don't feel the motion, it seems as if the Sun is moving and not us. The daily turning of Earth makes the Sun appear to move east to west across the sky.

- The daytime sky beyond the Sun is full of shining stars. We are blinded from seeing them because of the Sun's brilliance and the scattering of its light in our atmosphere.

FANTASTIC SUNSETS

Have you ever watched the setting Sun disappear over the horizon? The sinking Sun seems to grow bigger and wider and become many shades of red. Once it touches the horizon, it takes only two minutes to disappear. But the beautiful afterglow can last for half an hour or more before day fades into night. Actually, a fantastic sunset is a series of special effects caused by Earth's atmosphere.

- The setting Sun looks closer and bigger than usual — but it's not. When you see the horizon and the Sun at the same time, you think the Sun has enlarged. The same horizon illusion occurs with a rising full Moon.

- The setting Sun appears oval — but it hasn't changed shape. Light from the setting Sun comes in at a low angle. The air near the ground is dense and often polluted, so it bends, or refracts, the light, making the Sun look oval.

- Sunsets look red even though sunlight is a combination of all colors. When the Sun is low on the horizon, its light travels through more of Earth's atmosphere than when it shines from above. Along the way, the sunlight hits many particles in the air, which absorb or scatter its colors. Only red, orange and yellow penetrate through, giving the Sun its sunset color.

NIGHT SHADOW

After the Sun has set on a clear night, look eastward, away from where the Sun set. You may see a curved shadow moving slowly west across the sky. This shadow is called Earth's penumbra. It is cast on the sky by Earth as the Sun sinks farther and farther below the horizon. Once the penumbra covers most of the sky, you'll start seeing stars in the east and overhead. Finally, when there's no more afterglow from the sunset, you'll see stars everywhere.

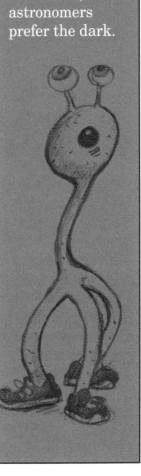

Q: How many astronomers does it take to change a light bulb?

A: None, astronomers prefer the dark.

MAKE A PLANISPHERE

A planisphere is like a 365-day map of the night sky. With this planisphere, you can track stars through the seasons. Some stars will set and disappear from the evening sky for months at a time, rising again later in the year. Others that seem to circle the North Star will be there every starry night. This planisphere is designed to find stars visible in the Northern Hemisphere.

You'll need:
paper
scissors
a ruler
a pencil
a paper fastener
tape

1.

Trace or photocopy the star chart on page 16. Trim into a circle.

2.

Trace or photocopy the horizon chart on page 17. Trim as shown to form direction pointers at the four corners.

3.

Cut small windows between 1 A.M. and 11 P.M., 7 P.M. and 5 P.M., 1 P.M. and 11 A.M., and 7 A.M. and 5 A.M., as shown.

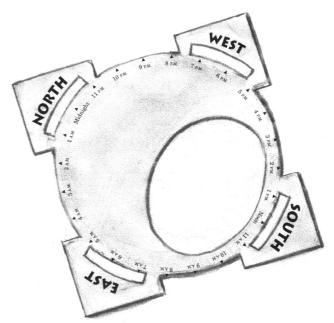

4.

Cut out the horizon window. If you live north of Seattle, Minneapolis, Montreal, Charlottetown or Paris, cut the horizon window 0.5 cm (¼ in.) more to the north.

5.

Place the star chart on another piece of paper and use a ruler to draw a square around it. Cut out the square.

6.

Center the star chart on the square and use a sharp pencil to poke a small hole through the middle of both layers at Polaris.

7.

Push the paper fastener through the hole and spread the fastener open.

8.

Place the horizon chart on top of the star chart and square, and tape it in place at the corners.

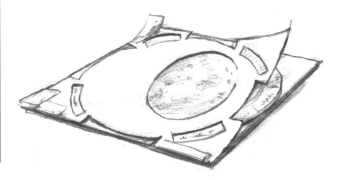

USING YOUR PLANISPHERE

1.

Find north using the Big Dipper (see page 9). Note a landmark that points north — the garage, the flagpole, etc. — for future nights.

2.

Line up the current time with the date. If it's daylight saving time where you live, set the dial back one hour.

3.

Hold the planisphere horizontally in front of you and face north. Turn the planisphere so that the north direction pointer is pointing to your stomach.

NORTH

4.

If you want to look for stars in the east, turn 90 degrees to the right and rotate the planisphere so east is pointing at you. South is 90 degrees more to the right and west is 90 degrees after that.

PLANISPHERE CHARTS

Trace or photocopy these charts to make the planisphere on page 14.

STAR CHART

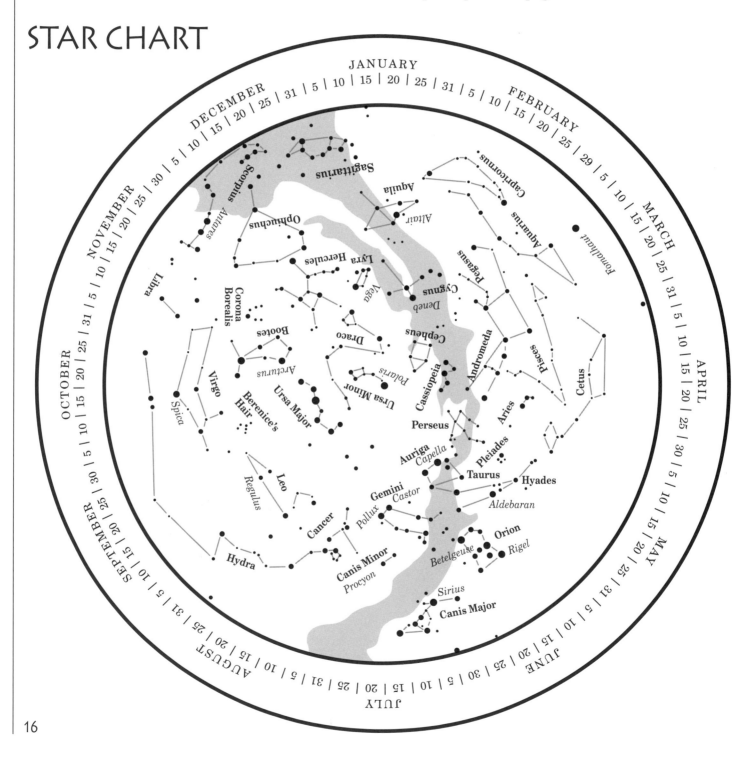

HORIZON CHART

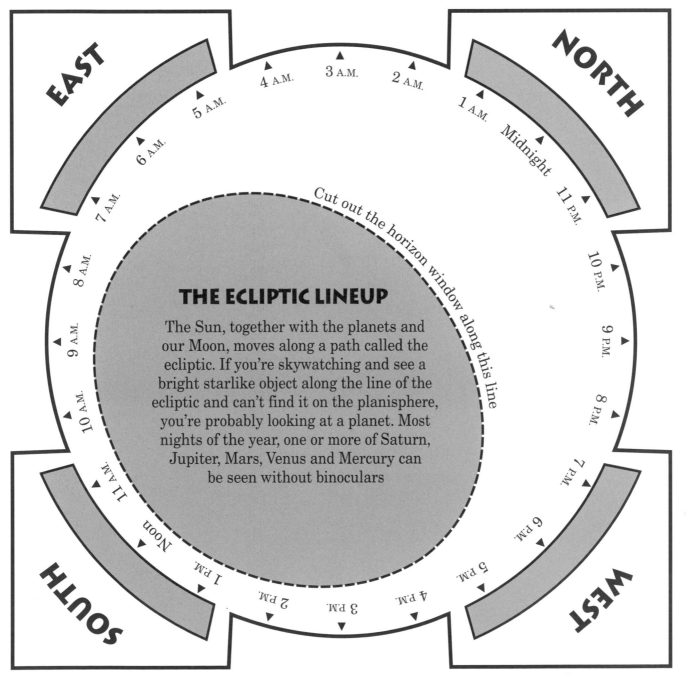

EAST

NORTH

WEST

SOUTH

4 A.M. 3 A.M. 2 A.M. 1 A.M. Midnight 11 P.M. 10 P.M. 9 P.M. 8 P.M. 7 P.M. 6 P.M. 5 P.M. 4 P.M. 3 P.M. 2 P.M. 1 P.M. Noon 11 A.M. 10 A.M. 9 A.M. 8 A.M. 7 A.M. 6 A.M. 5 A.M.

Cut out the horizon window along this line

THE ECLIPTIC LINEUP

The Sun, together with the planets and our Moon, moves along a path called the ecliptic. If you're skywatching and see a bright starlike object along the line of the ecliptic and can't find it on the planisphere, you're probably looking at a planet. Most nights of the year, one or more of Saturn, Jupiter, Mars, Venus and Mercury can be seen without binoculars

EQUIPPED FOR THE DARK

Make this red light and keep it with your skywatching equipment. Then you can check your planisphere, take notes in your astronomer's log and zero in on a biting bug without spoiling your night vision.

You'll need:
a small-beamed flashlight
a red sock, mitten, bandanna or piece of red cellophane
a thick elastic band or a piece of string

1.
Completely cover the end of the flashlight with the red material. Secure in place with the elastic band or string.

2.
Use your red light instead of a regular flashlight when stargazing.

ASTRONOMER'S LOG

For thousands of years, people have kept records about the sky. Shepherds watched for the seasons to change, sailors found their routes, astrologers predicted fortunes, and farmers planted their crops based on heavenly observations. Make this astronomer's log and keep track of what you see in the sky.

You'll need:
a spiral-bound notebook
a pencil
string
a ruler

1.

Tie a piece of string around the end of the pencil and secure it to the notebook's spiral binding.

2.

Use the ruler to divide the pages into columns. Label the columns "Date," "Time," "Place," "Aids" (telescope, binoculars, naked eye) and "Sightings."

3.

If you have a regular viewing spot, note a landmark, such as the sky above the spruce tree. Track the movements of the stars by recording what is visible in the sky in that spot each night you skywatch.

If you see something you can't identify, sketch it in your notebook and look it up later.

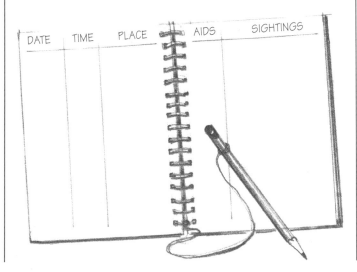

CHARIOT OF FIRE:
AN ACTION THRILLER

As morning turns to afternoon and then to evening, the Sun looks as if it's moving across the sky. We know it's really Earth that's moving and not the Sun, but ancient people believed what their eyes saw. The Greeks said the Sun was a god named Helios who drove his chariot every day from the eastern horizon across the sky to the west. Although they couldn't see Helios at night, they believed he continued to ride back under Earth to rise again the next morning in the east. This Greek story also mentions Ursa Major, the Great Bear; Scorpius, the Scorpion; Draco, the Dragon; Aquila, the Eagle; and the Milky Way.

Every morning, the Sun god, Helios, harnessed his four fiery horses to the chariot of the Sun. Then he set out on his daily journey across the sky to bring light and warmth to Earth below.

On one such ride, Helios looked down from the heavens and saw beautiful Clymene. He fell in love with her, and before long, Clymene gave birth to his son, Phaeton.

Phaeton grew to be a handsome and proud young man. Once, when he boasted that his father was a god, a friend sneered and challenged Phaeton to prove it. But Phaeton had only his mother's word, so he set out to find his father.

He walked east through the empires of the Ethiopians and Indians until he came to the Sun palace, glittering with its columns of gold and gates of silver. Phaeton strode right through the doors into the presence of Helios.

The Sun god recognized him, smiled radiantly and asked, "Son, why have you come here?"

Phaeton answered, "Great Helios, I have come looking for proof that I am your son."

"Ask me for anything you wish," Helios said, "It is yours."

Phaeton was ready with his answer: "Let me drive the Sun chariot for a day and steer your four winged horses on their course."

Helios regretted his promise and said, "I cannot take back what I have offered, my son, but I would like to change your mind. You haven't the experience or strength to control my fiery horses. Although you are my son, you are not a god. Heat from the chariot alone could kill you. The route is treacherous, reaching a dizzying height above Earth. One wrong move and you could be pulled backward with the sweep of the skies or dragged off course by

Story continued next page

ferocious beasts in the stars. Ask for anything other than this, my son."

But Phaeton's mind was set. Hoping to protect his son from the chariot's heat, the Sun god carefully washed Phaeton in holy oil. Then Helios placed his crown of golden sunbeams on Phaeton's head and said quietly, "The stars begin to fade and Earth looks for heat and light. If you are intent, go now."

Phaeton jumped onto the chariot and took up the reins. Helios held on to the bridle of one horse and gave his son a final warning: "Take care not to wander off course, but follow in my track. Don't use the whip — use your strength and wits to keep the horses in check."

When Helios let go, the horses leaped out of the palace gate and stormed through the purple clouds of dawn. They quickly outpaced the eastern wind as they strained into the steep climb toward the heavens. Never had Phaeton felt such power. But to the horses, the chariot felt light and the reins held no command. They jumped off Helios's well-worn track and started to blaze a new trail across the sky.

Phaeton tried reining in, but that made the horses more excited. The chariot swung wildly from side to side. Phaeton held on desperately, pushing down his growing fear. In high spirits, the horses pounded north and veered so close to the Great Bear that the beast grew hot and lunged toward the cool sea. Draco, the icy northern dragon, felt sudden warmth and lashed his tail at the chariot. Phaeton ducked, and when he dared stand up again, he had no idea where Helios's path lay. He wished he'd

never asked to drive the chariot, never even looked for his father.

The horses turned again. As they galloped past Aquila, the giant eagle tried to pluck Phaeton from the chariot with its sharp beak. The chariot swerved and Phaeton stared right into the evil eye of Scorpius, the Scorpion. When he saw the scorpion's stinger oozing deadly poison, Phaeton dropped the reins in terror.

Out of control, the horses dove toward Earth, scorching the land, burning great forests and drying up seas. Phaeton, overwhelmed by the heat and smoke, slumped into unconsciousness, his hands clamped onto the chariot's frame.

But the frenzied ride carried on. Whole cities burned as the chariot flamed above them. Gaia, goddess of Earth, cried out to Zeus and begged him to douse the fires. Because all the rain clouds had dried away with the heat, Zeus shot his deadly thunderbolt at the chariot, and the chariot exploded. Terrified, the horses bolted to Helios's western stables. Phaeton fell to Earth on the trail of a shooting star.

Helios was so saddened that he refused to repair or drive his chariot for one whole day, and Earth received neither heat nor light. Clymene searched until she found Phaeton's body, and she raised a gravestone for her son. Gaia's gentle tears slowly healed Earth, although the most severely scorched lands remain deserts to this day. Any night we see the Milky Way, the scar left by Phaeton's ride in the sky, we are reminded of that day when a boastful young man thought he could ride a god's chariot of fire.

OUR MOON

In this section, you can read an exclusive biography
of the Moon and get the inside scoop on its craters.
Demonstrate why the Moon seems to change from
a crescent to a circle, and learn to tell whether it is
waxing or waning by the direction the crescent faces.
Find out how the Moon eclipses the Sun, and try
to predict the occultation of a star. Then, help solve
the millennia-old mystery: does the Moon's face
look like a man, woman, rabbit or toad?

OUR MOON: THE OFFICIAL BIOGRAPHY

If the Moon could talk, how would it tell the story of its life? Let's follow its story from birth through teenage years to old age.

4.5 billion years ago: When the solar system is young, there is no Moon. Earth is still a molten blob orbiting the Sun. Then, a huge object the size of Mars hits Earth. The impact breaks off large sections of the planet. The chunks that hurl into space orbit Earth. Eventually, they are pulled together by the force of gravity to form the Moon.

4.4 billion years ago: Parts of the Moon's surface have cooled down enough to solidify into rock. But the solar system still has lots of rocky space debris left over from its formation, and the Moon's new crust is bombarded with fragments. When they hit the Moon, they cut wide craters, cracking the Moon's surface and creating deep fissures.

3.9 billion years ago: Now there are fewer large chunks of space debris left in the solar system to crater the Moon, but its surface continues to change. Hot molten rock from inside the Moon oozes out onto the surface lowlands and fills many craters. This lava hardens, creating dark, flat marks on the Moon's face known as seas.

3.2 billion years ago: The lava stops flowing. Little has happened on the surface since. Today, the Moon has no air, no water, no internal furnace and no life. It doesn't even shine by itself — moonlight is reflected sunlight. The Moon's surface changes so little that even a footprint left by an astronaut in the Moon dust will take millions of years to wear away.

27

THE EVER-CHANGING MOON

From Earth, the Moon is magical and mysterious. It seems to transform its shape, size and brightness from night to night. These changes repeat month after month in a pattern.

Every 29.5 days, the Moon seems to grow (or wax) from no Moon to a full Moon and then to shrink (or wane) to no Moon again. But the Moon doesn't really grow and shrink. The effect is created because the Moon orbits Earth while Earth and the Moon circle the Sun.

You and two friends can check out why the Moon seems to change shape and size. You, acting as Earth, stand in the middle of a dark room. One friend, Moon, walks in a circle around you, turning slowly so his face is always looking at you. Another friend, Sun, stands against a wall and points a flashlight at Moon. You, as Earth, look at Moon's face — depending on where Moon is in relation to you and Sun, part, all or none of his face will be in Sun's light.

The Moon is waxing when the crescent faces left. As it wanes, the crescent faces right. A waxing Moon is usually seen in the late afternoon or early evening sky, and a waning Moon after midnight and into morning.

MOON CYCLES

Each phase of the Moon's cycle has a special name:

Day 1
New Moon

Day 3
Waxing Crescent

Day 7
First Quarter

Day 10
Waxing Gibbous

Day 14
Full Moon

Day 20
Waning Gibbous

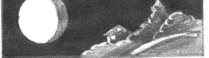

Day 22
Last Quarter

Day 26
Waning Crescent

REPEATING NURSERY RHYME

Jack and Jill went up the hill
To fetch a pail of water.
Jack fell down and broke his crown
And Jill came tumbling after.

This nursery rhyme may be connected to a Scandinavian myth about Hjuki and Bil, two children captured by the Moon. Their story is shown by the Moon's monthly cycle of waxing and waning. Look for the figure of Jack carrying his pail in the first quarter Moon. At the full Moon, Jill has joined Jack and they climb side by side, Jack on the right and Jill on the left. At the last quarter, Jack has fallen from view but you can still see Jill. By the waning crescent, she has disappeared, too.

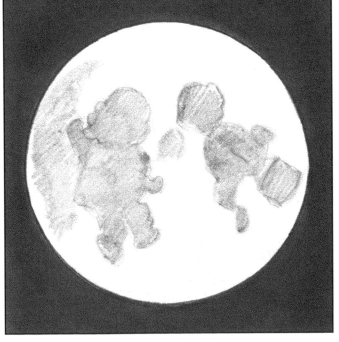

SUN'S DISAPPEARING ACT

An eclipse happens when one space object blocks the light reflecting from another space object. In the next eighteen years of your life, there will be forty-one eclipses of the Sun and twenty-nine of the Moon. In your lifetime, you may actually see only a few. Enjoy these unusual events more by knowing what to look for and how to view an eclipse safely. When the news tells you to expect an eclipse, you'll be ready.

A total eclipse of the Sun is an awesome event. The Moon moves between Earth and the Sun. The Moon's shadow sweeps across part of Earth, and daylight disappears for up to 7 minutes and 40 seconds. In that short time, birds roost in trees, the temperature drops, and night's brightest stars light up the sky.

Partial eclipses happen more often and occur when the Moon covers only part of the Sun.

Earth

Moon

Sun

PINHOLE ECLIPSE VIEWER

Viewing a solar eclipse is tricky. You can make this pinhole viewer to safely watch the whole show. **Never look directly at the Sun. Looking at the Sun is dangerous and may cause blindness.**

You'll need:

2 squares of stiff, white cardboard, 15 cm x 15 cm (6 in. x 6 in.)

a thumbtack

1.
Using the thumbtack, make a small hole in the middle of one piece of cardboard.

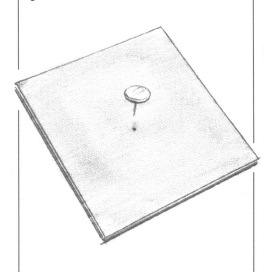

2.
Stand with your back to the Sun — outdoors or in front of a window — so sunlight shines over your shoulder. Hold the cardboard with the hole above the other piece.

3.
Position the hole until a spot of light shines through it onto the cardboard below. The closer together the cardboard pieces are, the brighter the image. The farther apart, the larger the image.

During an eclipse, you'll see an inverted image of the Sun on the lower piece of cardboard. You can watch the Sun disappear and reappear as the Moon moves across the Sun.

LUNAR ECLIPSE

Long ago, people watched the sky for signs of good and evil. Imagine what they thought when the Moon turned a dark and blotchy red. Death and disaster were sure to follow. Actually, they were witnessing a total eclipse of the Moon.

A lunar eclipse happens when Earth comes between the Sun and the Moon. It's Earth's shadow that makes the Moon appear red. The Sun and the Moon must be exactly opposite each other for a total eclipse — partial eclipses occur more frequently.

MAKE A LUNAR ECLIPSE

Try this experiment to simulate a lunar eclipse. Can you make a total eclipse?

You'll need:
a tennis ball
a Ping-Pong ball
a piece of wood, 1.5 m (5 ft.) long, such as an old hockey stick
glue
a large-beamed flashlight

1.

Glue the tennis ball (Earth) to one end of the stick and the Ping-Pong ball (the Moon) to the other end. Allow the glue to dry.

2.

In a dark room, or outside on a dark night, lay the stick on a flat surface. Shine the flashlight toward Earth (tennis ball). Is any light reaching the Moon (Ping-Pong ball)?

3.

Change the Moon's orbit by raising the stick at Earth's end. Shine the light from the same place. Adjust the stick's angle until the Moon is completely dark. Earth has totally eclipsed the Moon.

HIDE AND SEEK WITH THE MOON

Now you see it, now you don't. Wait, there it is again! Sometimes the Moon temporarily hides — or occults — a star, planet or satellite. When the Moon has completely passed the object, it will reappear. To see this in action, pick a bright star just west of the Moon. Watch closely with binoculars or a telescope. The star will disappear behind the Moon and then reappear within an hour on the other side.

How can an occultation occur when the Moon, stars and planets all move from east to west? Heavenly bodies move at different speeds, allowing the nearby Moon to overtake or pass in front of distant, slower-moving objects.

THE MOON IN THE BOG

Many people feel the Moon is a friendly face that watches over Earth. Sometimes it seems bigger and closer than other times. In this version of an old Irish story, we see what happened when the Moon got too close and, for a short time, was controlled by Earth's dark side.

In ancient Ireland, there were two villages connected by a path across an old, dry bog. At night, people had no fear walking across the bog to visit their neighbors. The clear gaze of the Moon lit the way and drove all the nasty creatures and evil spirits far into the surrounding countryside.

But one night the Moon wondered what the bog looked like up close. It flew down from its place in the sky and landed on the surface of the bog. Immediately the lurking nasty creatures and evil spirits jumped onto the Moon and covered it with dirt. They buried the Moon in the bog and rolled a huge stone over top to keep it there.

Then the nasty creatures and evil spirits roamed freely across the bog and into the villages. The people no longer visited their neighbors at night — there was no light and no safety from the dark forces.

After many nights of terror, the people in one village held a meeting to decide what to do. An old woman stepped forward and said, "If every person finds a small, smooth pebble and meets me at the outskirts of the village tonight, I will show you how we can overcome the nasty creatures and evil spirits."

The villagers agreed, and when they gathered at the edge of town that night, she told everyone to hold their pebble on their tongue and follow her quietly. The pebble would remind them not to break the silence by talking and alert the nasty creatures and evil spirits. She led the silent villagers along the path across the bog. When they reached the great stone, they rolled it away and scraped off the dirt beneath until they could see the Moon. When the Moon saw their faces, it jumped out of the bog and up into its place in the sky.

Ever since that night, the Moon has lit the bog with its friendly gaze, driving the nasty creatures and evil spirits far into the countryside. But the Moon shines from afar and is careful not to come too close to Earth again.

CHANG'O CHOOSES: A ROMANCE

When the Moon is full, especially at harvest time, young Chinese women remember the story of Chang'o. They scan the light and dark patches on the Moon's face for two of the creatures featured in her story — a rabbit and a toad.

The story says that long ago, Earth had ten suns not one. The suns were the children of the Jade Emperor and lived beyond the Eastern Ocean. The suns spent their days bathing and frolicking in the sea and took turns circling Earth to bring it light and heat. At night, like great dazzling birds, they roosted in the branches of an enormous tree.

One day the suns decided it would be fun to light Earth together, so all ten bounced into Earth's daytime sky. Their combined heat scorched the land — it melted rocks, dried up lakes, burned forests, shriveled plants and hurt all living things. But the suns didn't care. The Jade Emperor heard the cries of Earth's people and commanded the suns to stop their game, but the suns paid no attention. Even when the emperor raised his voice, they ignored their father.

The Jade Emperor turned to Yi, a god skilled in archery, to bring his unruly children under control. He gave Yi a magic bow and said, "Don't hurt the suns more than you have to — but stop their deadly game." Yi and his beautiful wife, Chang'o, traveled from heaven to Earth to carry out the emperor's wishes.

At first Yi tried to reason with the suns to stop their destructive game. But they said, "We're just having fun." Even when Yi threatened them with his magic bow, they wouldn't stop. Finally, Yi shot down one sun with an arrow. When the sun fell to the ground, it turned into a huge dead crow — and all Earth sensed a slight cooling. But the remaining nine suns refused to quit. Yi was so furious that he raised his bow and shot down one sun after another until only one remained. He would have killed the last sun had it not begged for its life.

The Jade Emperor was unhappy that nine of his sons were dead and would not allow Yi to return to heaven. He decreed that Yi and his wife would have to live, grow old and die as people. Yi begged the emperor to reconsider. Chang'o cried out, "It's not fair! Why am I punished for what my husband did?" But the Jade Emperor banished them both from heaven.

On Earth, Yi desperately tried to make his wife happy. He built a house in the mountains and hunted meat for their table. But Chang'o yearned for the palaces and fruits of heaven. Over time, Yi's hunting skills brought him wealth, and he was able to provide Chang'o with servants

Story continued next page

and a comfortable life. Yet she remained miserable, fretting about growing old and ugly.

One of their servants, Feng Meng, was jealous of Yi's success and his beautiful wife. He wanted to kill Yi but feared the magic bow. So he tried to trick Yi into destroying himself. Feng Meng told Chang'o about a pill that gave ordinary people immortality. It was made from a flower that grew beyond the mountains of Tibet. Feng Meng did not mention that the pill was owned by a monster goddess whose distant fortress was surrounded by a bottomless moat and a shield of flames.

Chang'o begged Yi to get the pill, and because he badly wanted to make his wife happy, Yi agreed to the journey. With great effort, Yi swam the moat and crossed the wall of flames. The goddess was so surprised to see him that she gave him her only pill — enough, she warned, for just one person to go to heaven or for two to live forever on Earth without aging or dying.

When Yi returned home, he and Chang'o agreed to share the pill at a special feast. In preparation, Yi told his wife he must go hunting;

instead, he went searching for the fruits she loved — melons, pomegranates, peaches and grapes. When he did not return quickly, Chang'o started to fret — she worried that the more she waited, the more her beauty and youth would fade. Then Feng Meng whispered in her ear that Yi wasn't going to come back. Chang'o was so upset she swallowed the pill alone.

Immediately, Chang'o started to float upward. She looked down to Earth and saw her husband on his way home, laden with her favorite fruits, and realized she had betrayed the man who loved her. She also sensed she would never be welcome in heaven. Chang'o looked for somewhere else to go and decided on the Moon.

Yi soon discovered that both his wife and the pill were gone. He looked up to heaven and saw Chang'o on the Moon. He lifted his bow to shoot her down — but then decided he loved her too much and broke his bow in pieces.

With the bow broken, Feng Meng lost his fear of Yi. He lay in wait for his master beside a footpath and killed Yi with a wooden stake. Chang'o saw her husband's murder and cried pitifully.

Some say the gods and goddesses were so angry they turned Chang'o into a toad. You can see a toad in the white shape at the bottom of the full Moon. Others say the gods and goddesses knew Chang'o had suffered in the loss of her husband and let her live in sadness on the Moon. Her only companion is a gentle rabbit whose shape can be seen in the dark patches of the full Moon.

NIGHTLY ATTRACTIONS:
THE STARS

In this section, you'll get starry-eyed. Gaze at faraway stars using your very own sighting tube. Find out the size and age of well-known stars, where they've been and where they're going. Then read their stories! Use a telescope or binoculars to spot complete constellations, from the obvious bright ones to the hard-to-find dim stars. And follow the Big Dipper's movements with an ordinary pizza tray or a star clock.

STARLIGHT, STAR BRIGHT

"**S**tarlight, star bright," the first star you see tonight will be a star that's close to Earth. In 150 B.C., a Greek astronomer named Hipparchus recognized that some stars appear brighter than others and organized a list of one thousand of the brightest stars seen from the Northern Hemisphere. Hipparchus rated the stars according to their magnitude (brightness) on a scale of 1 to 6, with 1 representing the brightest down to 6 for those barely visible to the naked eye.

In 1830, English astronomer John Herschel fine-tuned Hipparchus's scale and showed that 1st magnitude stars are about 100 times brighter than 6th magnitude stars. He also found that a few brilliant stars were too bright for Hipparchus's scale and added 0 and negative numbers to the scale. Herschel said that distant stars appear dimmer; closer stars appear brighter. For instance, Sirius, in the constellation Canis Major, is actually brighter than our Sun but it's much farther away from Earth. Sirius measures -1.4, and the Sun is a whopping -26.8.

BRIGHTEST STARS OF THE YEAR

Use a planisphere (see page 14) to locate the brightest stars in the night sky. It may take you a year to see them all!

Name of star	Constellation	Magnitude
1. Sirius	Canis Major	-1.4
2. Arcturus	Bootes	0
3. Vega	Lyra	0
4. Capella	Auriga	0
5. Rigel	Orion	0.1
6. Procyon	Canis Minor	0.3
7. Betelgeuse	Orion	0.7
8. Altair	Aquila	0.7
9. Aldebaran	Taurus	0.9
10. Spica	Virgo	1

★ ★

DISTANT CLOSE-UP

Try this easy experiment with a friend to show why distant stars appear dimmer than stars closer to Earth.

You'll need:
2 identical flashlights
a dark room

1.

Stand beside your friend about 1 m (3 ft.) from the wall (Earth) in a dark room. When your eyes are adjusted to the dark, shine the flashlights (stars) at Earth (the wall).

2.

One person takes a giant step backward. What do the star beams look like now?

3.

Repeat step 2 until you are standing as far away from each other as possible. The star closest to Earth will appear brighter than the other one. But you know the stars are equally bright, right?

Q: What kind of fish live in outer space?

A: Star-fish.

A STAR IS BORN

What a life! Begin with a bang, live for billions of years, swell into a red giant, shrink into a white dwarf and fade away. Read this personal interview with an aging star, then look in the sky and see all stars in a new light.

Q: I understand that your life began as a gas. Is this true?

A: Yes, darling, at least in part. Just like all stars, I began as a black swirling cloud of dust and gas particles in a star nursery, called a nebula. Finally my particles stuck together and grew hotter. When the temperature and pressure in my middle became high enough, huge amounts of energy began to flow outward toward the surface. I was now hot and bright enough to be called a star.

STAR NURSERIES

You can see a spectacular nebula in the constellation Orion (see page 108).

44

Q: How did you spend your youth?

A: Why, glowing, of course! Glowing night and day. I was a noticeable, but average, midsized yellow-white star. Hydrogen from my inner core fueled me into middle age.

Q: I hope this isn't a rude question, but are you creeping into old age?

A: Yes. Now I'm a red giant and these are my senior years. But I've lived nearly 10 billion!

Q: How did you become a red giant?

A: My hydrogen started running low and I had to burn the shell around my core. It's hard to see my various layers from Earth, but my core is shrinking and heating up at the same time as my shell layers are expanding and cooling. Compared to my younger days, I'm bigger and more bloated.

Q: So what's next?

A: When all the hydrogen in my core is gone, I'll burn helium first, then any fuel I have left. At that point, I'll be dying. But don't feel sorry. This could take another hundred thousand years or more.

Q: So that'll be it? You'll be finished?

A: I wouldn't say finished. I'd say beginning again. Part of me will become a small white dwarf and fade gently into the night. My remaining parts will end up in a nebula — where all stars begin life.

YELLOW STARS

The Sun is a familiar middle-aged yellow star, but it's easier on the eyes to look at yellow-white Procyon in the constellation Canis Minor or yellow Pollux in Gemini, the Twins constellation (see page 16).

COUNT YOUR LUCKY STARS

We can see only a small fraction of the estimated 400 billion stars in our home galaxy, the Milky Way. In perfect country conditions, a keen skywatcher can see as many as 3000 stars with the naked eye. A city dweller will be lucky to see more than 50 stars. Everyone can see more with the help of a telescope or binoculars!

THE TELESCOPE

Almost four hundred years ago, Dutch craftsmen experimented with mirrors, magnifying glasses and lenses and, by chance, developed the telescope. Try this experiment and see how it works.

You'll need:
a bathroom mirror
a magnifying glass
a pair of reading glasses

1.

Standing in front of the mirror, hold the magnifying glass at arm's length and look through it at your face. The magnifying glass collects light and bends it, so the image of your face is upside down.

2.

Now use the glasses as a diminishing lens or eyepiece. Hold one lens close to your eye and look through the magnifying glass. Adjust the distance of the magnifying glass and lens until the image of your face is both in focus and right side up.

A TELESCOPE FOR EACH EYE

"Bi" (two) and "oculars" (telescopes) put together mean a telescope for each eye. Hobby-quality binoculars are easier to use than a telescope and are great for bringing objects in the sky closer to you. For clear viewing, steady your elbows on a fence post, tabletop or other permanent fixture.

If your family has a telescope with a tripod base, ask an adult to help you set it up (see page 8). With a steady hand and practice, you'll see lots of stars that you can't see with your eyes and spot the dimmer stars that make up entire constellations.

AN INVENTION TO DIE FOR

Galileo heard about the Dutch telescope and made his own in 1609. With his telescope, he discovered the moons of Jupiter, the incredible surface of our Moon, sunspots and much more. He also became convinced that Copernicus's theory was correct — Earth revolves around the Sun, not the other way around, which was the common theory back then. The Church didn't agree and demanded, "Take back your words, Galileo, or face death by fire." But Galileo refused, and in 1633 the Church arrested him and confined him to his home, where he died nine years later.

MAKE A SIGHTING TUBE

Take a ride across the night sky without leaving your chair by using a simple sighting tube. Concentrate on your favorite constellation and watch as stars overhead enter from the east, move to the center of the tube and exit west. Your sighting tube will allow you to focus on a few stars at a time.

You'll need:

a cardboard tube with a diameter of 5 cm (2 in.), such as a paper towel tube
plastic-coated peel-and-stick shelf paper (optional)
a piece of wood, 3 cm x 2 cm x 65 cm (1 in. x ¾ in. x 26 in.), such as the handle of an old hockey stick
a measuring tape
a pencil
a hand saw
hockey or duct tape

1.

If you want to make the tube firm and longer-lasting, cover it with the shelf paper.

2.

Sitting in a chair, measure the distance from your eyes to your hips. Mark this distance from one end of the stick.

3.

Draw a 45-degree angle at the mark and have an adult saw along the line.

4.

Make a circle of tape and attach it to the angled end of the stick. Place the middle of the cardboard tube on the tape and press it in place.

48

5.
Secure the tube firmly to the stick by winding tape around both, as shown.

ANCIENT SIGHTING TUBES?

The Great Pyramid of Egypt, built more than 4500 years ago, has two narrow shafts extending from the interior main chamber to the outside walls. One shaft is directed toward Polaris, which is the only star in the night sky that does not seem to move. The other shaft lines up with Orion's belt (see page 108). The two shafts can't be sighting tubes because they aren't straight enough to see through. But we know Polaris and Orion were important to ancient Egyptians and the placement of the shafts probably had a purpose. Maybe they were reverse sighting tubes for the star gods to look into the pyramid and guard whoever was in there. Can you think of an explanation?

DATES AND STARS

Did you know you can use the night sky to tell the date? In fact, you can tell when your birthday is approaching just by looking at the night sky.

If you look at the stars an hour after sunset for a week, they may seem to shine from the same place. But if you look carefully, you'll notice that each night they shift slightly. Over the week, some stars in the west will disappear over the horizon, new stars will rise in the east, and the rest of the stars overhead will move a little in between. The changes follow a pattern that repeats each year. So, as your birthday approaches, the stars return to shine from the same place at the same time they shone on all your previous birthdays. Use your planisphere (see page 14) to tell where the brightest stars will be on your birthday and look for them in the night sky as your big day approaches.

In ancient times, people used the location of bright stars in the sky as a calendar.

- The early Egyptians noticed that the Nile River flooded once a year, moistening the dry desert soil. At the same time, the star Sirius returned in the east just before sunrise. So when Egyptian farmers saw that Sirius had returned, they knew it was a good time to plant their grain.

- Hundreds of years ago, Iroquois women who lived in present-day New York State planted their corn, bean and squash seeds every spring. For best results, they waited until the star Aldebaran had moved so far to the west that it was about to disappear for the summer.

WE NEED TO TAKE SIRIUS MORE SERIOUSLY!

DO THE STARS REALLY MOVE?

Earth not only spins once every twenty-four hours, it also orbits the Sun once a year. By day, we face the Sun, and by night, we face a section of the distant universe. As we travel along our orbit around the Sun, we see different sections of the universe. So each year, we orbit back, start over and see the same stars in their familiar places again. The movement of the Earth, not the stars, makes it look as if the stars move through a yearly cycle.

THERE THEY GO AGAIN!

- In midwinter, the Sun does not rise in the high Arctic. However, every December, the star Altair appears in the northeast at breakfast time. So the Inuit watched for Altair to time the "dawn" of their sunless winter days.

TIME FOR SCHOOL YET?

Q: What did the runner-up of the Miss Universe Pageant win?

A: A constellation prize.

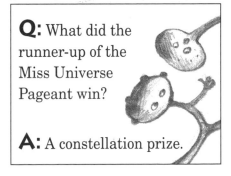

NORTHERN CAROUSEL

Every star in the night sky seems to move — except one. Polaris, our North Star, shines from the same place every night of the year. See for yourself. Find Polaris by following the pointer stars in the Big Dipper (see page 9). Then look at Polaris for a few minutes with your sighting tube (see page 48). If you keep your tube in one place, Polaris won't move out of range. But if you look at a star near Polaris with your sighting tube, that star will slowly move. The northern, or circumpolar, stars all turn in a counterclockwise direction around Polaris.

Polaris doesn't seem to move because it is almost directly above the North Pole. Earth spins every day like a carousel and Polaris lies directly over its center shaft. Try this activity to see how the circumpolar stars circle Polaris.

You'll need:

a round piece of cardboard, about 50 cm (20 in.) across, such as a pizza tray

a pencil and ruler

a bright yellow marker

a thin stick, about 30 cm (12 in.) long

1.
Find the center of the cardboard tray. Using the pencil and ruler, draw a line from top to bottom through the center. Draw another line from side to side at a right angle to the first line. Then draw two diagonal lines to divide the disk into eight equal sections.

2.
Using the marker, draw a star around the center point to represent Polaris. Poke the stick through the center point so the cardboard spins.

3.

In one section, draw the seven stars of the Big Dipper as shown.

4.

Directly across from the Big Dipper, draw the five stars of Cassiopeia, as shown.

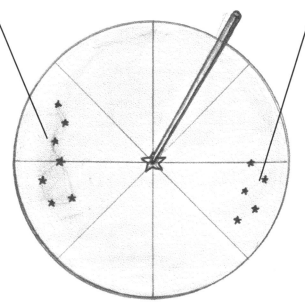

5.

Rotate the circle in a counterclockwise direction. You are imitating the movement of the northern stars and constellations around an unmoving Polaris.

THE SEASONS AND THE BIG DIPPER

If you live north of Philadelphia, Rome or Beijing, you can tell the season of the year by looking at the Big Dipper. Face north and look at Polaris. Your left shoulder points west, your right shoulder east and your back south. If it's before midnight in summer, the Big Dipper is to the west of Polaris, in autumn to the north, in winter to the east, and in spring to the south (or closest to overhead). For a modern explanation of why the Big Dipper seems to move with the seasons, see page 51. For an ancient explanation, see "Star Bear: A Hunting Adventure" (page 74).

MAKE A STAR CLOCK

The Big Dipper's circumpolar dance around Polaris, the North Star, is as predictable as clockwork, taking about twenty-four hours to complete one rotation. You can make a stellar timekeeper using Polaris as the middle, and the pointer stars of the Big Dipper as the clock's hand. The star clock runs on standard time. Add one hour for daylight saving time when necessary.

You'll need:
a square of stiff plastic, 15 cm x 15 cm (6 in. x 6 in.), such as the clear lid of a box
a permanent marker
scissors
a pen
a piece of white paper
a ruler
a small paper fastener

1.

Place the plastic sheet on the month and hour circle on page 55. Trace around it with the marker.

2.

Cut out the plastic circle. Use the pen to poke a small hole through the center.

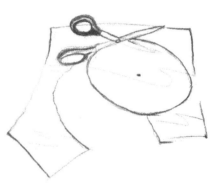

3.

Center the hole in the plastic disk over Polaris below and use the marker to trace the outline of the Big Dipper, Cassiopeia, the Little Bear and use the ruler to mark the arrow.

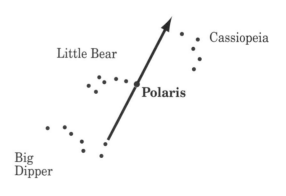

4.

Photocopy or trace the month and hour circle below onto a piece of paper. Cut out the paper circle and use the pen to poke a hole in the center.

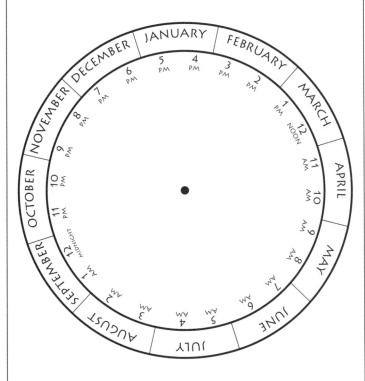

5.

Place the plastic circle on top of the paper circle and join them at the center with the paper fastener.

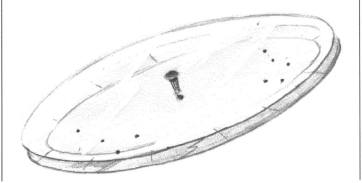

USING YOUR STAR CLOCK

On the next starlit night, take your star clock and red flashlight (see page 18) outside, and face north.

1.

Hold the paper disk with today's date at the top.

2.

Point the star clock toward Polaris, the North Star.

3.

Turn the plastic disk so the drawn constellations are in the same position as the real ones in the sky.

4.

Read the time indicated by the arrow.

THE ZODIAC

Imagine it's night and you're at sea in a small boat, far from land and without a compass. How will you find your way home? If you were an ancient Greek, you'd follow the zodiac.

The Greeks noticed that some stars move along the same east–west path at night that the Sun travels by day. They grouped these stars into constellations, which they named mostly after animals. And they called the whole band the zodiac, which means circle of animal signs. Greek sailors knew if they left home facing a rising zodiac constellation, they would get home by sailing toward a setting zodiac constellation.

You can also use the constellations to tell the season, unless you're in the Arctic or Antarctic, where the zodiac is hard to pick out. Look in the sky around 9 P.M. to see these constellations.

YOUR ASTRONOMICAL AND ASTROLOGICAL ZODIAC

Astrology or horoscope fortune-telling from the zodiac began with the Babylonians and reached its greatest popularity in Rome about two thousand years ago. Ancient astrologers said a person's sign was the constellation hidden behind the Sun on his birthday. But the twelve horoscope signs are not the same as the thirteen real zodiac constellations in the sky. The constellations are all different sizes and therefore hidden behind the Sun for different lengths of time, but horoscope signs are all the same size and last one month each. Turn to page 101 to find the real, astronomical zodiac constellation that coincides with your birthday.

TELLING THE SEASON FROM THE ZODIAC

SPRING

Cancer, the Crab; Leo, the Lion; and Virgo, the Maiden (see stories pages 68, 69 and 72)

AUTUMN

Capricornus, the Sea Goat; Aquarius, the Water Carrier; and Pisces, the Fish (see stories pages 100 and 101)

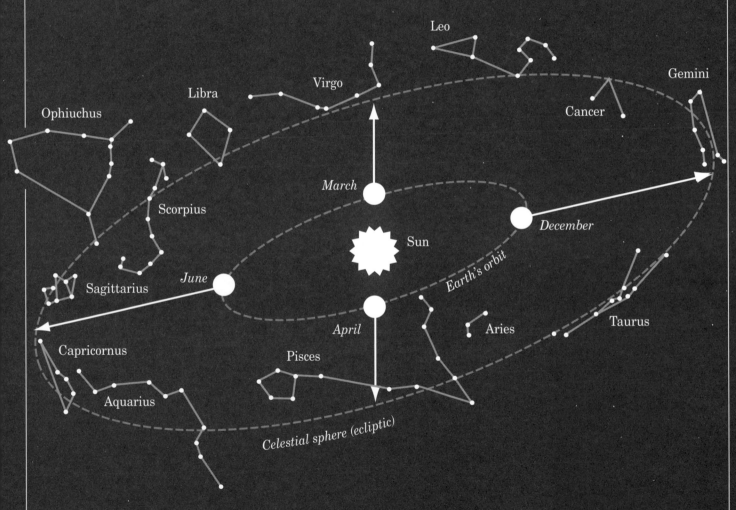

SUMMER

Libra, the Scales; Scorpius, the Scorpion; Ophiuchus, the Serpent Bearer; and Sagittarius, the Archer (see stories pages 20, 86 and 87)

WINTER

Aries, the Ram; Taurus, the Bull; and Gemini, the Twins (see stories page 118 and 119)

THE MAKING OF THE STARS

You know that stars are born in nebulae (see page 44), but if you'd lived a thousand or even a hundred years ago, your elders would have told another story. Here are two explanations for the existence of the stars. Both are out of this world!

A TALE FROM THE CÓCHITI INDIANS OF NEW MEXICO

Many years ago, a heavy rainfall and great flood forced a little girl named Blue Feather and her people to flee north. When the rain ended, Uresiti, the Mother leader of all Cóchiti, said they could return home. Uresiti asked Blue Feather to walk behind her people and carry a small sealed bag. Blue Feather knew it was an important package and must be kept closed.

With the bag strapped on her back, Blue Feather proudly trudged south, but soon she became curious. What could be inside such a small, light bag? The drawstrings were tightly knotted, but Blue Feather slowly untied them. All she wanted was a quick peek, but she was surprised to find thousands of stars inside the bag. Most of the stars escaped and flew into the sky, ending up wherever they pleased. Blue Feather tugged the strings shut and managed to trap a few. When she reached home, Uresiti named the remaining stars and carefully placed them in the sky where they belonged. These stars, such as those in the Big Dipper, are the friends of the Cóchiti people. The rest are nameless strangers.

BRIGHT EYES — A SCANDINAVIAN FOLKTALE

The goddess Idun lived with the other gods in a walled city called Asgard. There, she tended her magical fruit of eternal youth. Thjasse, a giant, kidnapped Idun, stole her magical fruit and went north. In Idun's absence, a terrible cold gripped the land, and without the fruit of youth, the remaining gods began to age and wither. To bring back good weather and their own strength, the gods sent Loki, god of fire, to save Idun and bring back the fruit.

Loki, disguised as a falcon, flew into Thjasse's palace and found Idun locked in a tower. He changed her into a nut, grabbed her in his talons and flew off toward Asgard. Thjasse turned himself into an eagle and chased after them. Meanwhile, the other gods prepared for Loki's return by stacking kindling and fuel around the edge of the city. When Loki and Idun landed safely within the city walls, the fires were lit. Thjasse, unable to stop, flew into the flames and died. His eyes were thrown into the sky, where they became thousands of stars.

NORTH

Cassiopeia,
the Queen

Cepheus,
the King

Draco,
the Dragon

Polaris

Ursa Minor,
the Little Bear

Auriga,
the Charioteer

Hercules,
the Strongman

The Big Dipper

EAST

Corona Borealis,
*the Northern
Crown*

Ursa Major,
the Great Bear

Gemini, *the Twins*

Bootes,
the Herdsman

Cancer,
the Crab

Berenice's
Hair

Leo,
the Lion

Milky Way

Virgo,
the Maiden

Hydra,
the Water Snake

SOUTH

SEASONAL ATTRACTIONS:

THE SPRING SKY

In this section, you will find out how to locate the spring constellations in the sky. Learn what's special about the equinox. Play Night Sky I Spy and other star-crazy games. And before the season is over, be sure to follow the adventures of Callisto, Hercules and chickadee as they stride, step and stalk, night after night, across the spring sky.

SKY MAP FOR THE EVENING HOURS

Turn the map so the direction you are facing is at the bottom.

WHAT TO LOOK FOR IN THE SPRING SKY

Once you locate the Big Dipper, you can use it to star hop and find the main constellations in the spring sky.

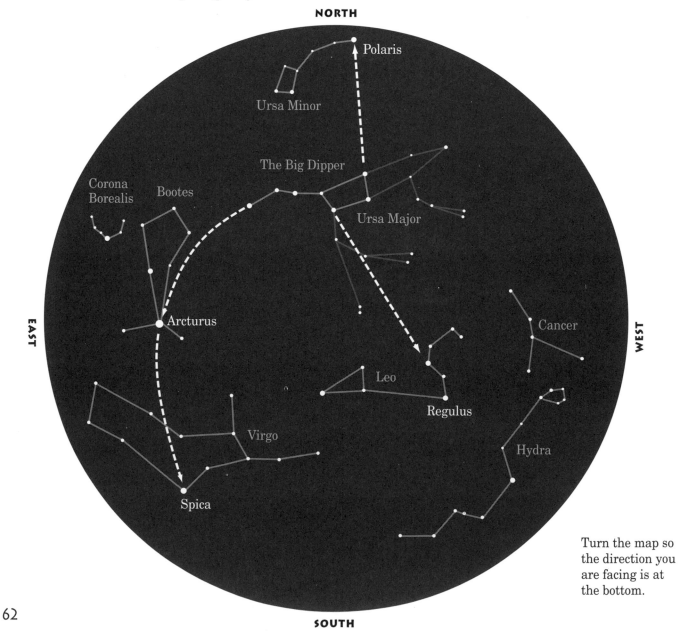

Turn the map so the direction you are facing is at the bottom.

URSA MAJOR, THE GREAT BEAR, AND URSA MINOR, THE LITTLE BEAR

Spring is the best time to find all the faint stars that make up the sky bears. The Big Dipper is a group of stars that form the Great Bear's hind end and tail. Polaris is the tip of the Little Bear's tail (see stories pages 20, 70 and 102).

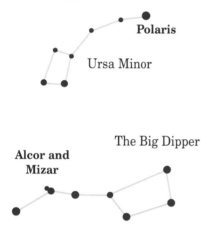

Polaris

Ursa Minor

The Big Dipper

Alcor and Mizar

ALCOR AND MIZAR

Look at the star second from the end of the Big Dipper's handle. Do you see two stars instead of one? Ancient Arabs used this double star as an eye test. They said if you could see dimmer Alcor as well as brighter Mizar, you had good eyesight.

ARCTURUS

The brightest star in the spring sky, Arcturus is found by following the arc of the Big Dipper's handle. Arcturus is a giant orange-yellow star near the bottom of the constellation Bootes, the Herdsman.

Bootes

Arcturus

CORONA BOREALIS, THE NORTHERN CROWN

By late spring, this small circlet of stars glitters east of Arcturus (see stories pages 74 and 134).

Corona Borealis

SPICA

From Arcturus, you spike south to Spica. Spica is the main star in Virgo, the Maiden (see story page 69), and one of the brightest stars in the spring sky.

Virgo

Spica

HYDRA, THE WATER SNAKE

This constellation's tail writhes south of Spica. Look for five bright stars close together under Cancer, the Crab, to find its head. Hydra may be faint, but it's the longest and largest constellation in the spring night sky (see story page 72).

Hydra

REGULUS

At the heart of Leo, the Lion (see stories pages 68 and 72), is the star Regulus, which is 150 times brighter than our Sun.

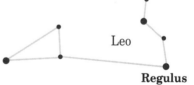

Leo

Regulus

Regulus is the dot in a group of stars that looks like a backward question mark — the head and mane of Leo, the Lion. The lion's hind end is a triangle of stars to the east of Regulus.

THE SPRING EQUINOX

There is one night in spring, usually March 21, when both night and day are exactly twelve hours long. On only one other day of the year does this happen — usually September 21.

An equinox is reached when the Sun crosses the celestial equator, an imaginary line across the sky directly above Earth's equator. If you were to stand on Earth's equator at noon on the equinox, you would cast no shadow. The Sun rises directly in the east and sets directly in the west at the equinox.

THE MOON AND THE EQUINOX

Because the Moon usually travels along the same path as the Sun, look for these special effects of the Moon at the spring equinox.

- At the equinox, the Moon climbs into the sky at its steepest angle of the year. That means it quickly rises above the glow of sunset and light pollution, so it can be seen more clearly and earlier than usual. If the Moon is just past new, look for its thin crescent shape right after sunset.

- If the Moon is a waxing crescent, look at the part not lit by the Sun. The equinox is the best time to see the glow of earthshine, when sunlight reflecting off Earth hits the Moon and bounces back. On Earth, we can actually see the Moon's face even though it is in shadow. And with this added earthshine, the sunlit crescent seems larger and brighter, too. People say, "The old Moon is in the new Moon's arms."

SHADOW PLAY

The Maya of Central America were fascinated with the equinoxes. They constructed the Temple of Kukulcán at Chichén Itzá so the late-day Sun on March 21 and September 21 creates a zigzag pattern of light and shadow down one staircase. The pattern looks like a diamondback rattlesnake. Sure enough, at the base of the staircase, a stone-carved snakehead sits in full light at sunset.

The Anasazi people of New Mexico found natural places where the Sun creates special effects on the equinox. In Chaco Canyon, they marked a shaded rock wall that only one sunbeam reaches — and only on the equinoxes in March and September. They drew a spiral on the wall, so the sunbeam looks like a dagger approaching a bull's-eye at noon on the equinoxes.

65

STAR GAMES

Play these wacky star games any time of year and turn that big black and white sky into your own private playground.

NIGHT SKY I SPY

Test your knowledge of what's in the night sky and challenge your friends' knowledge, too.

1.
Whoever goes first finds a constellation, star or planet and says, for example, "I spy Venus."

2.
The player who points out Venus adds another challenge, for example, "Can you see the Big Dipper?"

3.
Whoever finds the Big Dipper says, "I spy the Big Dipper. Can you see ..." Continue until you have spied everything you can identify in the sky.

THEN ALONG CAME ...

Create your own way-out stories from the sky with a little help from a planisphere (see page 14). This storytelling game can be played indoors or out.

1.

Look at a planisphere and pick a constellation that interests you. It helps to choose a constellation named after an animal or a famous person, such as Scorpius or Hercules. Write your selection on a piece of paper.

2.

Set the planisphere so your constellation is on the eastern horizon. Rotate the dial by two hours and choose a second constellation that rises later — Aquila, for example. Add it to the list. Continue around the planisphere until you have twelve constellations.

3.

The storyteller who wants to begin tells a tale about the first constellation. When he's finished his part, he introduces the next constellation by saying, "Then along came ..."

4.

The second storyteller names the second constellation and continues the tale, weaving in whatever comes to mind about her constellation.

5.

Continue until all twelve constellations have had their stories told.

I PACKED MY BAG FOR THE UNIVERSE

Try playing this familiar ABC game with a universal twist. Use names of constellations, planets, asteroids, galaxies and crazy made-up alien names (very handy for X, Y and Z)!

1.

Sitting in a circle, choose someone to start. She begins by saying, for example, "I packed my bag for the universe and in it I put Aquarius."

2.

The next person says, "I packed my bag for the universe and in it I put Aquarius and Bootes."

3.

Continue through the alphabet, using all previous names, until you can't remember a name or you reach Z, whichever comes first.

SPRING ZODIAC STORIES

LEO, THE LION

There is no mistaking the outline of the noble lion in the constellation of Leo. He boldly faces west, crouched and ready to pounce. Ovid, a Roman poet, wove this tragic tale around the pose of Leo.

Pyramus and Thisbe lived side by side. They were in love but their parents would not allow them to marry. All they could do was whisper to each other through a hole in the wall between their houses. One day, they planned a secret meeting at the edge of a white mulberry grove. Thisbe arrived first and was horrified to find a lion devouring its prey. As she ran away to warn Pyramus, her silk scarf fluttered to the ground near the lion. He swatted it away, covering it in blood. When the lion had his fill, he sauntered off.

Soon, Pyramus arrived at this grisly scene and immediately saw Thisbe's scarf covered in blood. Assuming his loved one had perished in the jaws of the lion, he flung himself on his sword and died. Thisbe returned and found Pyramus's body. She kissed him for the first and last time and then stabbed herself with his sword. Their blood entered the roots of the mulberry, whose fruit has been red ever since.

Jupiter placed Thisbe's scarf in the sky as Berenice's Hair, a wispy constellation that floats near Leo.

VIRGO, THE MAIDEN

The leading lady of the zodiac constellations, Virgo has been seen throughout history as a woman holding a sheaf of grain. To the Chaldeans, she represented Ishtar, a goddess with powers over fertility and crops.

Ishtar was married to Tammuz, the harvest god, and together they oversaw a bountiful world of plenty. But then the King of Winter defeated Tammuz in battle and dragged him off to the underworld. Ishtar wept and moaned and completely forgot about the crops. Finally, she decided to follow Tammuz into the underworld, where she, too, was captured. The plants withered, and winter took hold of the land. The gods in the sky saw the desperate conditions on Earth and asked the guard of the underworld to release Ishtar and Tammuz. Since then, Virgo has dominated the sky during spring planting.

BIG DIPPER STORIES

The Big Dipper is easy to spot overhead on a spring evening. And because it's the most recognized star grouping in the Northern Hemisphere, there are many Big Dipper stories and legends.

CALLISTO THE BEAR

As in many cultures, the Greeks saw the Big Dipper as part of a larger constellation shaped like a bear.

According to legend, the all-powerful god Zeus fell in love with Callisto, a beautiful huntress. Zeus's wife, Hera, was so jealous that she changed Callisto into a bear. Now the young huntress was prey, lurking in the woods hiding from hunters.

One day, Callisto heard her son Arcas's voice and raced to greet him. Terrified by the sight of a roaring she-bear on her hind legs, Arcas raised his bow and took aim. At the last second, Zeus saved Callisto by changing Arcas into a little bear. He swung them both by their tails, flinging them into the sky. Since then, mother and cub have been united as Ursa Major and Ursa Minor. Hera, furious that Zeus still cared for her rival, banished the bears to the cold North Pole among constellations that never set.

THE WATER DIPPER

This Philippine folktale highlights the dipper in the Big Dipper.

Terrible times fell on the village of a poor woman and her son. The hot weather dried up the wells, people became weak and sickly, and the woman lay on her bed gasping. She begged her child for water — even a few drops to wet her tongue.

The boy took a water dipper made from a coconut shell and ran from the house, but everywhere was dry and he became discouraged. Looking to the sky, the boy asked to be guided to water. Instantly, water gushed from the ground where the boy stood. He filled the dipper, gave thanks to heaven and started for home. An old man called out, asking for a sip. The boy stopped, let the old man drink and dashed off toward home.

In his hurry, the boy tripped and fell, spilling the water and smashing the dipper. He sat down and sobbed. Then, looking to heaven again, he asked once more for water. Where he had spilled from his dipper, a well appeared.

Shouting with excitement, the boy called the other villagers to come and drink their fill. He borrowed another coconut shell and filled it with water for his mother. When he looked to heaven again, his broken dipper was being lifted skyward and turned into the stars of the Big Dipper.

HERCULES VS. HYDRA

Are you ready for the greatest championship event of all time? Hercules, the Strongman, takes on Leo, the Lion; Hydra, the Water Snake; and Cancer, the Crab. In this yearly replay, watch Hercules beat his legendary foes night after night, from east to west across the sky.

Hercules was the son of Zeus and an earthly princess. Zeus's wife, Hera, grew fiercely jealous of the princess and placed two poisonous snakes in Hercules' cradle. But even as an infant, Hercules had superhuman powers and squeezed the vipers to death with his bare hands. When he became an adult with children of his own, jealous Hera tried to destroy Hercules again, this time by driving him insane. Out of his mind, Hercules mistook his sons for ferocious wild animals and killed them. When he regained his senses, Hercules asked the Oracle at Delphi how he could make up for his terrible crime. The Oracle told him to complete twelve labors set by the King of Mycenae.

The first task the King set was to kill the Nemean Lion. This beast had such thick skin no weapon could pierce it. Hercules fought the lion for thirty days and finally squeezed it to death in a wrestling hold. Then Hercules skinned the lion and made himself a cloak no weapon could pierce. When he was finished, he hurled the lion into the sky, where it is to this day.

The king was not pleased. He set a harder task for the second labor — to kill Hydra in the marshes of Lerna. This creature was a dreaded nine-headed water snake that was so poisonous people died by inhaling its stench. Hercules took a deep breath and charged at Hydra with his knife. But every time he cut off a head, two more grew on its bloody neck. So Hercules set the end of his club on fire and burned each neck stump to stop the heads from growing back.

When Hera saw that Hercules was about to defeat Hydra, she sent a giant crab to harass him. But Hercules trampled the crab to death at the same time that he cut off the last of Hydra's heads. Victorious, Hercules dipped his arrows in Hydra's blood. Now, with poisoned arrows and his lion skin cloak, the strongman was more invincible than ever.

Strangely enough, although Hercules completed all twelve labors, he died as a result of Hydra. One of his enemies gave a vial containing Hydra's poison to Hercules' wife, who, thinking it was love potion, covered his robe with it. The poison burned Hercules' skin so painfully he begged Zeus for help. Zeus sent a cloud to Earth and lifted Hercules into the sky, where you can still see his figure among the stars.

HEADS UP

Use your planisphere (see page 14) to see how long it takes Hercules to kill Hydra, the Water Snake. Start in the spring, when Hydra is in view and Hercules first rises. Turn the planisphere ahead to the date when the last of Hydra's heads disappears in the west and Hercules is left victorious, in center sky.

STAR BEAR: A HUNTING ADVENTURE

Long ago, the Micmacs of northeastern North America watched the Big Dipper circle the North Star every year. They used the different positions taken by the circumpolar stars, starting in the spring, to tell the story of a bear hunt. The bear is the bowl of the Big Dipper. Her seven hunters, all birds, are the three handle stars of the Dipper plus four stars in Bootes, the Herdsman. The bear's den is Corona Borealis, the Northern Crown.

In early spring, a keen-eyed chickadee spotted a bear climbing out of her winter's den. The chickadee knew he couldn't take on the bear alone and called his six friends for help — two owls, a blue jay, a passenger pigeon, a gray jay and a robin. The bear caught a glimpse of the hunters and ran for her life. The chase began.

Through all of spring and summer, the hunters tracked the bear across the night sky. In early autumn, the two owls, clumsier fliers than the rest, dropped out of the chase and fell below the horizon. As the nights grew colder, blue jay and pigeon lost the trail and disappeared. Gray jay, chickadee and robin

managed to keep up the chase but grew thin with hunger. In mid-autumn, robin finally cornered the bear. The bear rose up on her hind legs in self-defense, but robin stood his ground and shot her with an arrow. Bear fell on her back and died.

Overcome with hunger, robin jumped onto the bear for a quick bite of fat and was smeared in blood. He flew to a nearby maple tree and tried to shake it off. The blood splattered far and wide, turning the maple leaves red. One patch of blood would not shake off and it stained robin's breast forever.

Finally chickadee caught up with robin. Together, they started a fire, carved up the bear and cooked the meat. When they were ready to eat, gray jay arrived and demanded his full portion. Chickadee and robin were happy to share. While chickadee stirred the pot, gray jay and robin danced around the fire. The hunters were thankful for the food.

The bear's skeleton lies on its back all winter while her spirit moves into another bear asleep in the den. Ever since, when spring returns, a new bear climbs out and the hunt starts all over again.

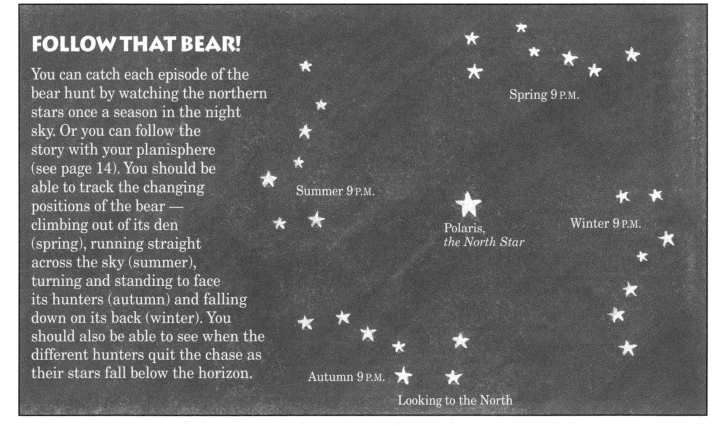

FOLLOW THAT BEAR!

You can catch each episode of the bear hunt by watching the northern stars once a season in the night sky. Or you can follow the story with your planisphere (see page 14). You should be able to track the changing positions of the bear — climbing out of its den (spring), running straight across the sky (summer), turning and standing to face its hunters (autumn) and falling down on its back (winter). You should also be able to see when the different hunters quit the chase as their stars fall below the horizon.

Spring 9 P.M.

Summer 9 P.M.

Polaris, *the North Star*

Winter 9 P.M.

Autumn 9 P.M.

Looking to the North

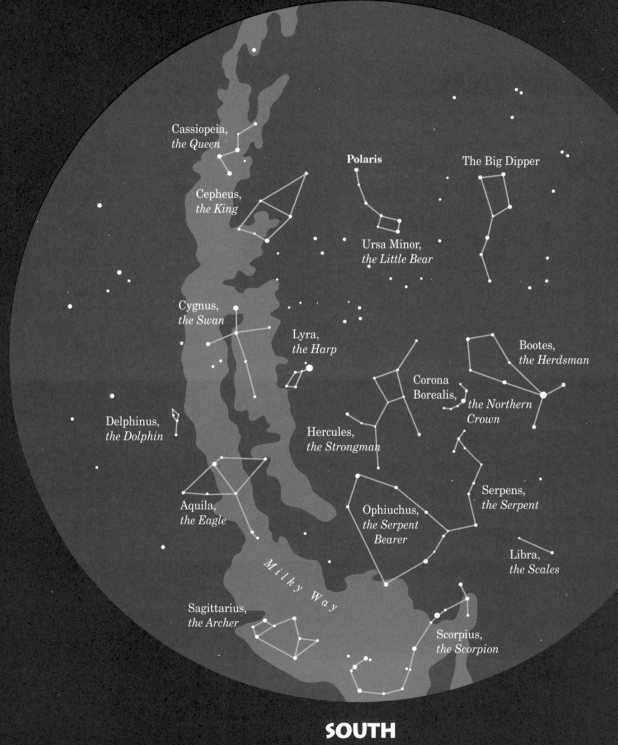

EAST

Cassiopeia,
the Queen

Cepheus,
the King

Polaris

The Big Dipper

Ursa Minor,
the Little Bear

Cygnus,
the Swan

Lyra,
the Harp

Bootes,
the Herdsman

Corona
Borealis,
*the Northern
Crown*

Delphinus,
the Dolphin

Hercules,
the Strongman

Serpens,
the Serpent

Aquila,
the Eagle

Ophiuchus,
*the Serpent
Bearer*

Libra,
the Scales

Milky Way

Sagittarius,
the Archer

Scorpius,
the Scorpion

SOUTH

SEASONAL ATTRACTIONS:
THE SUMMER SKY

Summer nights are short, so you'll have to stay up late to see all the night sights. Get to know the giant Summer Triangle, featuring Vega, Altair and Deneb. On a clear, dark night, bedazzle your friends with a meteor shower celebration. Discover the enormity of your home galaxy — the Milky Way. You decide: is the Milky Way a pathway for warrior ghosts or a river in the sky?

SKY MAP FOR THE EVENING HOURS

Turn the map so the direction you are facing is at the bottom.

WHAT TO LOOK FOR IN THE SUMMER SKY

Your hosts of the summer sky are three bright stars — Vega, Altair and Deneb. Together they make up the Summer Triangle. Look for the triangle in the east on a June evening, moving to overhead as the season progresses.

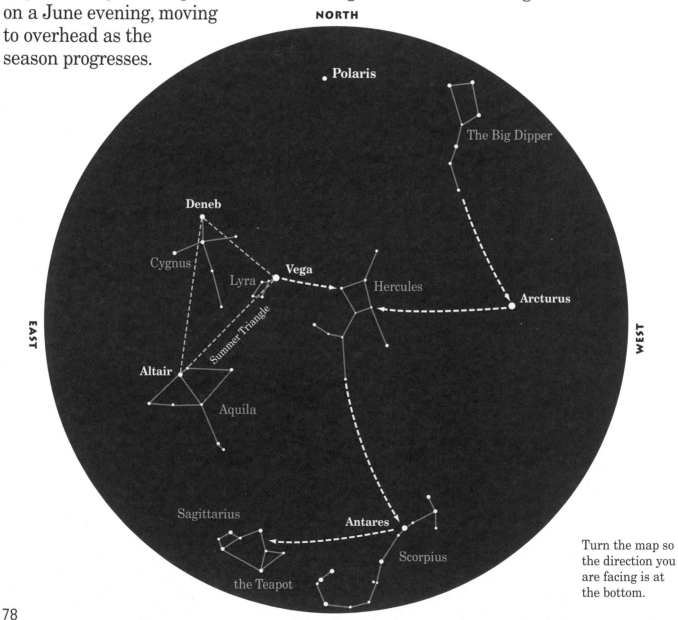

Turn the map so the direction you are facing is at the bottom.

VEGA

The brightest star in the Summer Triangle, Vega is bluish white. It is in the constellation Lyra, the Harp (see story page 88).

ALTAIR

The second-brightest star in the triangle, Altair is white. Altair is in the constellation Aquila, the Eagle (see stories pages 20 and 88).

DENEB

The dimmest star of the Summer Triangle, Deneb would be the brightest if it were not so far away. It is actually 60 000 times brighter than our Sun. Deneb is the tail of the large constellation Cygnus, the Swan (see story page 136). The head of Cygnus lies between Altair and Vega. Some people call Cygnus "the Northern Cross."

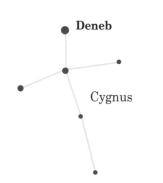

Once you have found the Summer Triangle, you can star hop to find …

THE KEYSTONE

Between Vega and Arcturus, look for four stars in a wedge or keystone shape. This is the body of Hercules, the Strongman (see story page 72). His feet are to the north and his arms to the south, making his figure kneel upside down in the sky.

Keystone

Hercules

ANTARES

Look directly south of Hercules, almost to the horizon, to find the supergiant orange-red star Antares, the heart of Scorpius (see stories pages 20 and 86). Farther south and east of Antares, look for the creature's nasty hooked stinger.

THE TEAPOT

To the east of Scorpius but still well to the south, look for the outline of a teapot in the sky. The stars that make the teapot also make the eye, bow and arrow of Sagittarius, the Archer (see story page 87).

Sagittarius

THE SUMMER SOLSTICE

Every day from late December to June, the Sun rises and sets a little farther north along the horizon. But about June 21, the Sun seems to stop moving north. It rises in the northeast and sets in the northwest, seemingly in the same spots for several days. After the pause, the Sun travels south to reach another standstill, or solstice, on or about December 21. Earth's elongated orbit around the Sun plus the tilt of Earth's axis produces the standstill effect. At each solstice, Earth is rounding one of the long ends of its orbit. As we swing around the end, neither Earth nor the Sun seems to move. The same standstill effect occurs when you toss a ball in the air. The ball seems to freeze at the top of your throw before it falls back down.

CELEBRATING METEORS

Summer is a great time to wake up your family and friends to the wonders of the mighty meteor (see page 133). You'll need a late bedtime — the show doesn't get rolling until after ten and goes into the wee hours of the morning.

PARTY DATES

Most nights you'll see about six meteors shoot by in an hour. But six times a year, the sky erupts with as many as a hundred meteors an hour (see the box on page 81). Some meteor showers last a few nights; others are a one-night show. Check a calendar or newspaper for a day when there will be no Moon or just a sliver during a meteor shower. You'll see more meteors on a dark night.

Most meteor showers are named after the constellation they seem to radiate from. Lie down and point your feet toward this "home" constellation and then look in that area.

With a friend, follow these instructions to see even more meteors. The example used here is for the Perseid meteor shower in August.

1.
Locate Perseus, just east of Cassiopeia. One person looks for all meteors to the left of Perseus, the other to the right. Call out when you see one, and keep track of how many each person sees.

2.
After five minutes, compare counts. If few meteors have been seen, one spotter looks above Perseus, one below. When you locate the part of the sky with the most meteors per minute, focus on that area and enjoy the rest of the show.

Q: Where did the astronauts park their spaceship?

A: At a parking meteor.

Meteor shower	Location	Home constellation	Dates
Quadrantids	Northeast	Draco	January 3
Eta Aquarids	East	Aquarius	May 1–9
Delta Aquarids	Southeast	Aquarius	July 25–31
Perseids	Northeast	Perseus	August 10–14
Orionids	East	Orion	October 19–24
Leonids	East	Leo	November 16
Geminids	East	Gemini	December 10–14

THE MILKY WAY

The Milky Way, our home galaxy, is made up of about 400 billion stars. It spins through the universe like a giant pinwheel with long spiral arms that arch away from a star-packed central bulge. Our Sun is more than two-thirds out from the center of the galaxy on one of its arms.

From Earth, the Milky Way looks like a misty band of light in the night sky. In summer, Earth faces the middle of our galaxy, so the Milky Way is brighter than at any other time of year. The center of the galaxy is in the direction of the spout of the Teapot in Sagittarius. If you look there, you'll see patches of dust and gas so thick they block out the starlight shining behind them. Many of these dust clouds, or nebulae, are nurseries where stars are being born.

HUBBLE'S OWN TELESCOPE

Astronomer Edwin Hubble proved that the Milky Way was not the only galaxy in the universe. He photographed the Andromeda Galaxy with a telescope and showed it was made up of billions of stars, just like our Milky Way.

THE HISTORY OF OUR GALAXY (AND THE UNIVERSE, TOO)

The distant past: The whole universe may be smaller than the head of a pin. Who knows? Space and time don't exist — yet!

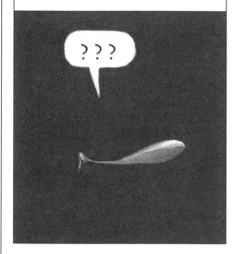

About 13 billion years ago: The universe expands rapidly outwards. Space and time begin.

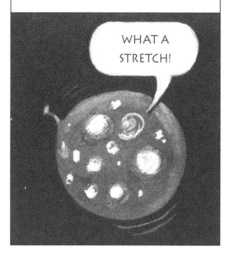

... a few seconds later: The whole universe is a raging fireball, filled with hot, glowing, colliding electrons, protons and photons.

... 300 000 years later: The temperature in space cools and hydrogen atoms form. Space becomes transparent for the first time.

Up to the present: Gas and dust swirl through space, sometimes collecting into large clouds and collapsing to form stars, planets and even galaxies like our Milky Way.

Distant future: Will the universe, time and space grow forever or end in a big crunch?

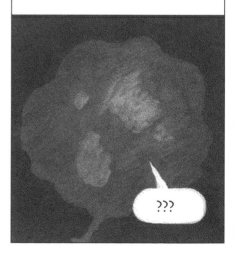

MILKY WAY STORIES

In 1609, Galileo pointed his telescope on the Milky Way and discovered it was made up of millions of stars. Today, scientists think migrating birds use the light from these stars to navigate. The Estonians of Northern Europe have an old tale that links migrating birds to the Milky Way.

Lindu, beautiful daughter of the sky god Uko, took care of all birds on their spring and fall flights. Many young men wanted to marry her, but Lindu found none as exciting as her birds.

North Star was the first to propose. He arrived in a fine carriage drawn by six dark horses and laden with ten gifts. But Lindu was not interested because she knew he preferred to stay in one place all the time. Then Moon pulled up in his silver coach with ten horses and twenty gifts. But Lindu turned him down because he traveled along the same, well-worn path every night. When Sun appeared in a golden chariot drawn by twenty strong red horses and thirty gifts, Lindu rejected him, too. She knew Sun walked the same old path Moon did, except by day. Lindu found all the young men boring.

Then Northern Lights drove up in a diamond carriage drawn by a thousand white horses and carrying gifts beyond counting. He was brash and brilliant; he came and went as he pleased. Dazzled, Lindu fell in love. Northern Lights told her to prepare for their wedding and that he would return — and then he disappeared into the north.

Lindu put on her bridal dress and waited … through autumn, winter, spring and into next summer. She stared north, growing more and more unhappy, never thinking of her friends the birds. As autumn approached again, Uko felt he must do something to help his daughter and the birds. He called upon the wind to carry Lindu into the sky. There she remains, her long, white veil shimmering as the Milky Way, directing the birds in their journeys. But she stares north, trying to catch a glimpse of Northern Lights. When she sees him, she waves. And occasionally he waves back.

A WELL-LIT ROAD

The idea that the Milky Way's band of light was a "way" or road runs through many old stories.

- The Norse of Scandinavia said the Milky Way was the path that warrior ghosts traveled to reach Valhalla, their afterworld.

- The Yup'ik of eastern Siberia and western Alaska said the Milky Way was the snowshoe track left by Raven after he created people.

- The Armenians said the Milky Way was a trail of straw dropped by a thief.

- Some ancients said the Milky Way was a celestial waterway. The Egyptians called it a heavenly Nile River, the Hindus a Ganges River in the sky and the Hebrews a river of light.

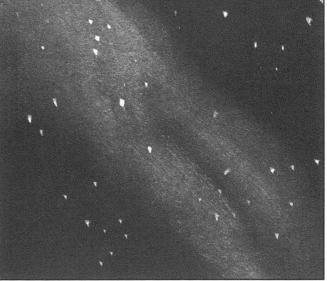

♈ ♉ ♊ ♋ ♌ ♍ ♎ ♏ ♐ ♑ ♒ ♓

SUMMER ZODIAC STORIES

LIBRA, THE SCALES

About 237 B.C., the ancient Greeks created a new constellation called Libra, the Scales, by taking the scorpion's claws from the constellation Scorpius.

At that time, the Sun passed into Libra at the autumn equinox, when each day was half light and half dark. The Scales were in perfect balance.

Libra, the Scales, is close to the constellation Virgo, which some ancients saw as Astrea, the goddess of justice, with scales in one hand and a sword in the other. Astrea used the scales to "weigh" a person's character and decide if he was good or bad.

SCORPIUS AND OPHIUCHUS

Real-life scorpions are nocturnal creatures that hide in deep cracks and strike prey or intruders with their tails. In this story involving the constellations of Scorpius and Ophiuchus, the scorpion's sting prevents Orion from killing the creatures of Earth.

Orion, son of Neptune, the sea god, was so tall he could walk in the sea and still keep his head above the waves. He was also powerful and fearless. Once he boasted he could kill all the animals in the world. Gaia, the goddess of Earth, feared he might actually do it and sent a scorpion to kill Orion. The scorpion's sting severely wounded the hunter and it took Ophiuchus, the most famous doctor of ancient times, to nurse him back to health.

You can watch Orion's story unfold on your planisphere (see page 14). He hunts across the evening sky from November to April.

♈ ♉ ♊ ♋ ♌ ♍ ♎ ♏ ♐ ♑ ♒ ♓

But when Scorpius rises in the east, a wounded Orion disappears in the west. Later, when it's Scorpius's turn to set, look for Ophiuchus, the Serpent Bearer, just above, ready to trample the scorpion. In the fall, Scorpius disappears in the west and Orion rises in the east again, healed and ready to hunt.

SAGITTARIUS, THE ARCHER

Sagittarius was a centaur — a creature that was half man, half horse. The Romans named him Chiron and claimed he named all the constellations in the sky.

Tales of Sagittarius focus on his ability as a hunter poised and ready to shoot from the middle of the Milky Way. Supposedly he shot his arrow at Taurus. When the bull retreated below the horizon in the northwest, the victorious archer appeared in the southeast. On dark August nights, follow the path of Sagittarius's arrow to Antares, the red star known as the scorpion's heart. Sagittarius is shooting Scorpius because it poisoned Orion.

THE WEAVER PRINCESS AND THE HERDSMAN: A ROMANCE

In this ancient Chinese story, the Milky Way is a silver river whose rushing waters separate two lovers. Standing on one side is the weaver princess, the star Vega. On the other is the herdsman she loves, the star Altair.

Long ago and after a hard day's work, a lonely herdsman and his old ox rested in the shade beside a stream. Seven beautiful sisters appeared and, not seeing the herdsman, bathed in the water. The herdsman was dazzled by the beauty of the youngest but was too shy to stand up and speak to her.

The old ox whispered to the herdsman, "She is the weaver princess — the one who weaves the clothes of the gods. If you hide her robe, she will be unable to fly back to heaven. Then she will be your wife."

The herdsman was surprised to hear the ox speak, but took its advice. While the princess searched for her hidden robe, her sisters dressed and flew away. Then the herdsman stepped forward and gently offered his coat to the princess. She was grateful and soon agreed to become his wife.

In time, the herdsman and the weaver princess had two children. The princess was happy and forgot about her work in heaven. But when the gods needed new clothes, the goddess Queen Mother found the princess's weaving loom quiet. Queen Mother's heavenly guards took three years to find the weaver princess. When they did, they carried her back to heaven.

The herdsman and his children were desperately lonely for the princess. But the old ox again spoke: "I will die soon. When I do, cut off my hide and wear it over your shoulders. It will take you to your wife."

The herdsman was sad to lose his old friend the ox, but followed its advice. The herdsman put his children in buckets on either end of a pole, then placed the pole across his shoulders and the ox hide over his back. Immediately, he rose to heaven and the family was reunited.

Once again the weaver princess stopped weaving. When Queen Mother saw the weaving loom quiet, she took a silver hairpin and drew a line across heaven. Water gushed into the line and formed a silver river that separated the herdsman from his wife and children.

Both the herdsman and the weaver princess wept bitterly. Eventually, their sadness touched the heart of the King of Heaven and he ruled they could spend one day a year together — on the seventh day of the seventh month. He said all the magpies in the world would form a bridge of wings for them to cross the silver river for their short reunion.

If it rains on July 7, people say the weaver princess is weeping tears of joy to be with her husband again. If the night is clear, people look at the stars and think of the faithful love of the separated couple.

Among the fainter stars that twinkle near Vega and Altair, look for the children of the weaver princess and the herdsman. Some people even see two buckets, a herdsman's staff and a weaving shuttle.

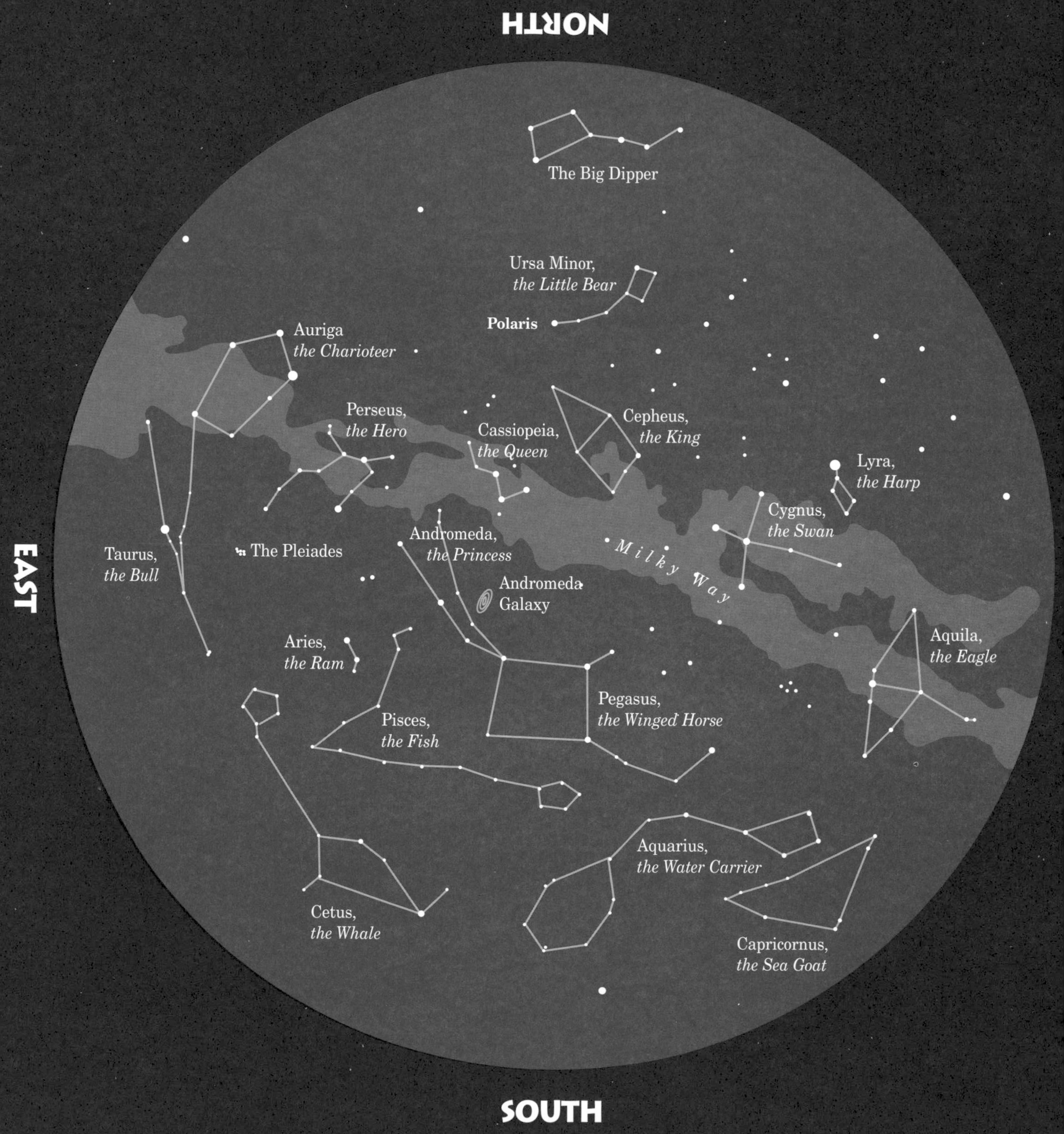

The Big Dipper

Ursa Minor,
the Little Bear

Polaris

Auriga
the Charioteer

Perseus,
the Hero

Cassiopeia,
the Queen

Cepheus,
the King

Lyra,
the Harp

Cygnus,
the Swan

Milky Way

Taurus,
the Bull

✺ The Pleiades

Andromeda,
the Princess

Andromeda
Galaxy

Aquila,
the Eagle

Aries,
the Ram

Pisces,
the Fish

Pegasus,
the Winged Horse

Cetus,
the Whale

Aquarius,
the Water Carrier

Capricornus,
the Sea Goat

EAST

SOUTH

SEASONAL ATTRACTIONS:

THE AUTUMN SKY

In this section, find out how to locate the stars and constellations in the autumn sky. Before the Sun goes down, get ready by having a celestial scavenger hunt. Clear, crisp autumn nights are great for finding northern lights and searching for distant galaxies. If it's rainy, make a night sky dome and decorate it with characters from your favorite sky story. Complete the season with stories of the zodiac, the Little Dipper and Perseus.

SKY MAP FOR THE EVENING HOURS

Turn the map so the direction you are facing is at the bottom.

WHAT TO LOOK FOR IN THE AUTUMN SKY

Get acquainted with the constellation Cassiopeia, the Queen, and she'll lead you to most of the famous stars and constellations in the autumn sky. You can see Cassiopeia all year round, but in autumn she takes center stage.

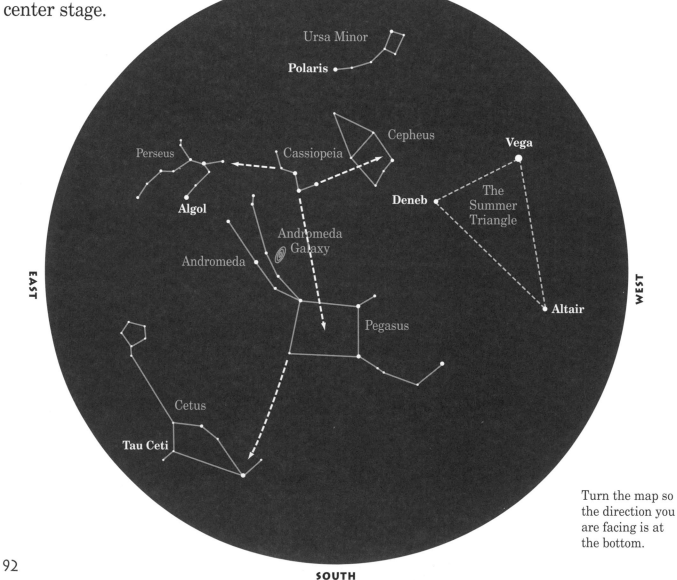

Turn the map so the direction you are facing is at the bottom.

CASSIOPEIA, THE QUEEN

To find Cassiopeia in the fall, face north. This circumpolar constellation looks like an M or a W. The Summer Triangle lies to the west of Cassiopeia, Ursa Minor, the Little Dipper, farther north and the Milky Way stretches east–west across the sky in a band that goes through Cassiopeia.

Cassiopeia

PERSEUS, THE HERO

Follow the Milky Way east from Cassiopeia to find Perseus. Algol, the most southwesterly star in Perseus, is actually a double star — two close stars that circle and eclipse each other every three days.

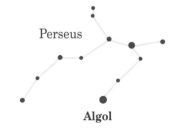

Perseus

Algol

CEPHEUS, THE KING

West of Cassiopeia, you'll see a group of stars that looks like a house. As night deepens, Cepheus, the King, leads Cassiopeia, his Queen, across the sky. Turn to page 104 to read a story that links Cepheus, his Queen and all the major autumn constellations.

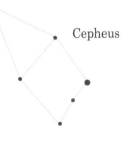

Cepheus

PEGASUS, THE WINGED HORSE

Look for four stars in a square south of Cassiopeia. This is the Great Square of Pegasus, the body of the horse. When you look through the square, you are looking beyond the Milky Way galaxy.

Great Square of Pegasus

THE ANDROMEDA GALAXY

Our nearest galaxy neighbor lies between Cassiopeia and Pegasus. It looks like a hazy smudge in the sky. The Andromeda Galaxy is a spiral galaxy like our own, but it's larger. The constellation Andromeda, the Princess, lies below the galaxy in a V of stars that starts at one corner of the Great Square of Pegasus.

CETUS, THE WHALE

South of Andromeda, near the southern horizon, look for the monstrous whale. Scientists think one of the fainter stars in Cetus, Tau Ceti, is so similar to our Sun that it's a good place to begin a search for extraterrestrial life!

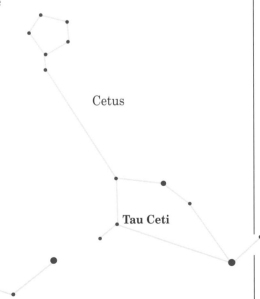

Cetus

Tau Ceti

MAKE A NIGHT SKY DOME

In the Middle Ages, Europeans used to paint night sky scenes on the domed ceilings of their buildings. You can make a night sky dome to hang in a window or from your ceiling and see your favorite constellations indoors, day or night.

You'll need:

a large plastic bowl
petroleum jelly, such as Vaseline
125 mL (½ c.) flour
15 mL (1 tbsp.) salt
250 mL (1 c.) water
a spoon
newspaper, torn into strips 1 cm (½ in.) wide
scissors
poster or tempera paints, including black
a paintbrush
white glue (optional)
thread

1.
Turn the bowl upside down and thinly coat the outside with petroleum jelly.

2.
In another container, mix flour, salt and water to make a smooth, runny paste. (Covered with plastic wrap, this paste will last in the fridge for a few days.)

3.
Dip the newspaper strips into the paste one at a time, using your fingers to spread the glue evenly. Place the strips on the bowl to cover it, overlapping the strips and smoothing the paste as you go.

4.
Repeat step 3 to make four layers, placing the strips in a different direction for each layer.

94

5.

Near the lip of the bowl, poke a small hole in your dome. Let your work sit for several days, until completely dry.

6.

When dry, the dome should easily lift off the bowl. Once separated, wipe any petroleum jelly off the dome with a damp, soapy cloth. If the dome's lip is rough, trim it with scissors, rub paste along the lip and lay a newspaper strip along the paste. Smooth your repair with paste and let it dry.

7.

Paint the outside of the dome any color you like and let it dry.

8.

Paint the inside of the dome black and let it dry.

9.

Paint white or yellow stars inside the dome for your favorite constellations. When dry, brush with a thin layer of glue for a glossy finish, if you like.

10.

Tie thread through the hole you made in step 5. Hang your night sky dome from the ceiling.

CELESTIAL SCAVENGER HUNT

Here's a fun game to play 'til the stars come out. Gather friends or family and create a scavenger hunt with a theme that's out of this world.

1.
Decide if this hunt will happen indoors, outdoors or both. With the help of an adult, determine what places are unsafe or off-limits and declare them out of bounds. Keep clear of streets, water and cliffs.

2.
Divide the group into two teams, each equipped with a pencil and paper and a shopping bag.

3.
Set a time limit. For a one-hour hunt, make a list of about twenty items to collect. See the box on page 97 for ideas. Include difficult-to-find things as well as easy-to-find things. All items must be borrowed with permission or found.

4.
At the end of the hunt, teams present what's been scavenged. They take turns showing and telling — trying to convince the other team that each item is really what they say it is. The other team decides which items are worth a point, and may award bonus points for amazing originality. The team with the most points wins.

SUGGESTIONS FOR SCAVENGER LIST

- an extraterrestrial creature
- a night light
- astronaut food
- a piece of a meteorite
- a big dipper
- stardust
- Moon boots
- a flying saucer
- a black hole
- Orion's belt
- a red giant
- Saturn's ring
- a boy from Mars
- a girl from Venus
- a cow that jumped over the Moon
- Zeus
- a solar reflector
- a celestial sphere
- Sagittarius's arrow
- Newton's apple

THE NORTHERN LIGHTS

On crisp, clear nights in fall or winter, keep your eyes on the northern sky. If you notice a greenish glow, you may be in for a display of northern lights.

WHAT CAUSES THE NORTHERN LIGHTS?

Electrically charged particles constantly stream toward Earth from the Sun in the solar wind. Earth's magnetic field deflects most of these particles back out into space. But some particles slip through the magnetic field, escape, dive toward Earth and enter our atmosphere near the North and South Poles.

When these particles strike air molecules, faint jolts of light energy are released. When sunspots form on the Sun (see page 11), more electrically charged particles flood into our atmosphere and more collisions occur, and the northern lights grow bigger and clearer.

WATCH FOR THE NORTHERN LIGHTS TO GROW MORE SPECTACULAR IN STAGES:

1. The green glow takes the shape of a long, arcing ribbon of light.

2. Vertical rays flicker along the ribbon.

3. The ribbon starts to flap and fold as if it's blowing in a breeze.

4. The ribbon widens and lengthens, forming gigantic curtains of light that sway side to side and sometimes change colors.

OLD EXPLANATIONS FOR THE NORTHERN LIGHTS

- In stories told by Inuit elders, the northern lights are spirits playing football in the sky. The players use a walrus skull for the ball.

- In Maine and New Brunswick, Passamaquoddy elders tell of a game of lacrosse in the land of the northern lights. The players wear lights on their heads and rainbows around their waists.

- To some Siberians, the northern lights are ghost warriors replaying old battles in heaven.

- For the Saami of northern Europe, the northern lights are spirits of the dead lighting up the sky with a message of hope — spring will come again.

- The Shetland Islanders of northern Scotland call the northern lights "the merry dancers."

99

♈ ♉ ♊ ♋ ♌ ♍ ♎ ♏ ♐ ♑ ♒ ♓

AUTUMN ZODIAC STORIES

CAPRICORNUS, THE SEA GOAT

Capricornus, seen low in the southern sky in autumn, forms a triangle as it straddles the ecliptic. The Greeks used to say these faint stars represented Pan, the god of music and nature.

Pan, a cheerful satyr (half man, half goat) was playing the panpipes when a hideous hundred-headed monster named Typhon surprised him and the other gods of Olympus. Pan dove into the river and tried to transform into a fish. In his panic, only his hindquarters became fishlike; his head and torso remained those of a goat. Unable to flee, Pan clawed his way onto shore in time to see Typhon tearing Zeus's limbs from his body and hurling them away. All Pan could do was scream, but the noise attracted Hermes, who collected Zeus's scattered body parts. Pan and Hermes put Zeus back together, and as a reward, Pan's sea-goat shape was preserved forever in the constellation Capricornus.

AQUARIUS, THE WATER CARRIER

Most recorded histories of Aquarius describe a man pouring water from a jug. In dry areas, he was a hero bringing precious water. But people of other areas claimed he caused floods and drowned crops.

In Greek mythology, Aquarius, also known as Ganymede, was extremely good looking. Zeus — fascinated with his beauty — sent the eagle Aquila to carry Ganymede to the heavens. Ganymede became Zeus's personal cupbearer, pouring him water and wine. Zeus's family was jealous of their close friendship, but that didn't stop Zeus from giving Ganymede his own constellation. Aquarius, guarded by Aquila, the Eagle, on his east, pours water onto a brilliant bluish-white star called Fomalhaut.

♈ ♉ ♊ ♋

PISCES, THE FISH

Venus and her son Cupid were playing along a riverbank when the fierce and invincible giant Typhon took them by surprise. Thinking quickly, Venus grabbed Cupid and plunged into the river — she knew Typhon could not survive in water. Venus and Cupid transformed into fish connected by a fishing line so they would never lose each other. They remain that way to this day in the constellation Pisces.

WHAT'S YOUR CONSTELLATION?

Everyone has an astronomical zodiac constellation that coincides with her or his birthdate. What's your constellation (see page 57)?

Constellation		Your birthday	Best night viewing
	Aries	April 19–May 13	October–February
	Taurus	May 14–June 19	October–March
	Gemini	June 20–July 20	December–May
	Cancer	July 21–August 9	January–May
	Leo	August 10–September 15	February–June
	Virgo	September 16–October 30	April–June
	Libra	October 31–November 22	June–July
	Scorpius	November 23–November 29	July–August
	Ophiuchus	November 30–December 17	July–August
	Sagittarius	December 18–January 18	July–August
	Capricornus	January 19–February 15	August–October
	Aquarius	February 16–March 11	August–October
	Pisces	March 12–April 18	October–January

LITTLE DIPPER STORIES

The Big Dipper outshines the Little Dipper. But during autumn evenings, the Little Dipper (Ursa Minor, the Little Bear) is higher in the sky and easier to see than the Big Dipper. The Little Dipper shares most stories with the Big Dipper, but these are a few of its own.

The famous sixteenth-century German mapmaker of the cosmos, Petrus Apianus, didn't see a bear in the Little Dipper. He thought these seven stars were the nymph daughters of Atlas, the great Titan. They lived on Mount Atlas, where they grew and tended the tree of the golden apples. Mother Earth gave this tree to Zeus when he married. The apples were the fruit of everlasting life, and only gods were allowed to pick them.

Egyptian skywatchers saw a giant hippopotamus in the Little Dipper. Because the northern stars never set, the Egyptians were superstitious about them and thought they might be evil. It was the strong hippo's job to circle the North Pole and keep order among the other circumpolar stars. As well, the hippo gobbled up all dead people who had lived wicked lives.

YOU NAME IT!

The Little Dipper has been called many names over the millennia. Which do you like best?

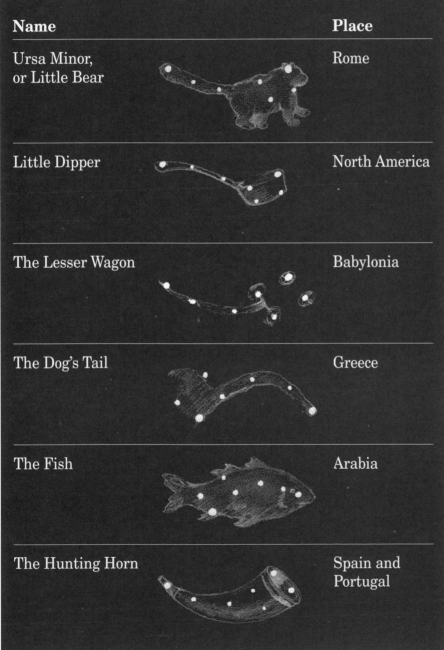

Name	Place
Ursa Minor, or Little Bear	Rome
Little Dipper	North America
The Lesser Wagon	Babylonia
The Dog's Tail	Greece
The Fish	Arabia
The Hunting Horn	Spain and Portugal

DIPPERS FLYING HIGH

In 1926, Alaska had a contest to decide the design for its state flag. A thirteen-year-old boy named Benny Benson combined the stars of the Big Dipper and the Pole Star in the Little Dipper on a dark blue background. This flag has been waving over Alaska ever since.

THE ADVENTURES OF PERSEUS: AN ACTION THRILLER

The ancient Greek story of Perseus is a true blockbuster. The hero travels across many lands in a lifetime of adventure. Several constellations in the autumn sky are named after characters in his story — Pegasus, the Winged Horse; Andromeda, the Princess; Cassiopeia, the Queen; Cepheus, the King; and Perseus, the Hero.

Perseus's adventures began before he was born. An oracle told Perseus's grandfather, the King of Argos, that he would die at the hand of a future grandson. To keep his daughter, Danae, from ever having this child, the king shut her in a tower. But mighty Zeus loved Danae and entered her window as a golden rainshower. When she gave birth to Perseus, the king dared not kill Zeus's son. Instead, he sealed mother and child in a chest and threw them out to sea. After drifting for days without food, they were found by a fisherman on the shore of a distant island.

Several years later, Polydectes, ruler of the island, asked Danae to marry him. When she refused, Polydectes tried to carry her off, but Perseus, now grown, stood in his way. So Polydectes devised a scheme to get rid of Perseus. He invited all the young men on the island to a feast. The guests were expected to bring gifts. Because he had nothing to give, Perseus offered to perform a feat of Polydectes' choice. Polydectes was ready with his answer: "Bring me the head of Medusa."

Perseus realized he'd been tricked. No one had ever faced Medusa and returned alive. She had writhing snakes for hair, tusks like a pig, brass scales on her hands and neck, huge wings and, worst of all, the power to turn into stone anyone who looked at her eyes. She lived with her two monster sisters, but no one knew where.

Zeus saw that Perseus was in a desperate situation and sent two gods to help his son. Athena gave Perseus a shield polished like a mirror. Hermes handed him a sword that could cut metal. Hermes took Perseus to find the Nymphs of the North, who possessed three magic items needed to behead Medusa — a cap of invisibility, winged sandals and a magic bag.

Perseus put on his winged sandals and flew west until he found Medusa's island. He spotted Medusa and her sisters asleep among their victims' stone bodies. Carefully looking into her reflection in Athena's shield and not at Medusa herself, Perseus dove down and cut off Medusa's head with Hermes' sword. As he picked up the head, the snakes hissed in Medusa's hair and

Story continued next page

Pegasus, the Winged Horse, burst out of her neck. Medusa's sisters woke up, but Perseus threw her head in his magic bag, pulled on the cap of invisibility and rode off on Pegasus.

On the way back to Polydectes' island, Perseus and Pegasus flew over the Kingdom of Ethiopia. Looking down, Perseus saw the beautiful Princess Andromeda by the seashore — but a giant sea monster was swimming close by. Perseus and Pegasus swooped down to warn Andromeda, only to discover she was chained to the rocks. Perseus tried to break the chains with his hands, but he could not.

"Stand back or you, too, will die!" Andromeda cried out.

"I will not leave," Perseus replied. "Why are you chained here?"

Andromeda said her mother, Queen Cassiopeia, had angered the gods by boasting she was more beautiful than even the nymphs of the sea. As punishment, the gods sent a sea monster to terrorize the kingdom. King Cepheus decided to appease them by sacrificing his daughter. Andromeda's husband-to-be refused to defend her, so she faced the monster alone.

After Andromeda finished her story, Perseus said, "I will save you and you will be my bride." With that, the monster reared up from the sea, and Perseus thrust Hermes' sword into the beast's mouth. As it died, the sea turned red with the monster's blood. Then Perseus cut Andromeda's chains with the sword and carried her to the Ethiopian palace.

King Cepheus and Queen Cassiopeia welcomed the couple. But Andromeda's former fiancé arrived with armed followers and demanded his promised bride. The king and queen cowardly agreed and told Perseus to leave. Perseus asked Andromeda to shut her eyes, then he opened his magic bag and held Medusa's head high. Everyone but Andromeda and Perseus turned to stone.

Perseus married Andromeda and took her to Polydectes' island. He found his mother, Danae, and the old fisherman in hiding because the ruler had tried to force Danae to marry him again. Perseus left Andromeda with his mother and entered the palace. Polydectes demanded that Perseus leave.

"I have brought what you wanted," Perseus said. With that, he pulled Medusa's head from the bag, and Polydectes and his friends instantly turned to stone.

The islanders were happy to be free of their ruler. They asked Perseus to be their king, but he said no. He wanted to return to Argos, the land of his birth. When his grandfather heard that Perseus was returning, he fled Argos, and Perseus was named king.

In the years to come, Perseus competed in games of strength all over Greece. One day he was throwing the discus in a faraway city when it slipped and killed an old man watching the games. As it happened, the man was Perseus's grandfather. The prediction of the oracle had finally come true — the old King of Argos died at the hand of his grandson, Perseus.

Many years later, when Perseus and Andromeda had also died, Zeus put them into the heavens along with Pegasus, Queen Cassiopeia and King Cepheus so people would remember all the parts of Perseus's fantastic story.

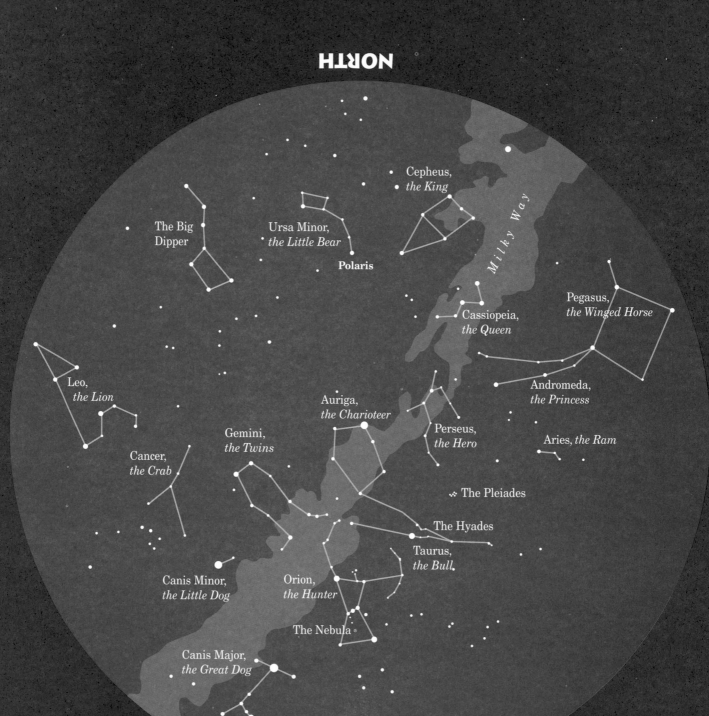

EAST

Cepheus,
the King

The Big
Dipper

Ursa Minor,
the Little Bear

Polaris

Milky Way

Cassiopeia,
the Queen

Pegasus,
the Winged Horse

Leo,
the Lion

Andromeda,
the Princess

Auriga,
the Charioteer

Perseus,
the Hero

Aries, *the Ram*

Gemini,
the Twins

Cancer,
the Crab

The Pleiades

The Hyades

Taurus,
the Bull

Canis Minor,
the Little Dog

Orion,
the Hunter

The Nebula

Canis Major,
the Great Dog

SOUTH

SEASONAL ATTRACTIONS:
THE WINTER SKY

Some of the brightest stars of the sky shine on winter nights: Aldebaran, Procyon, Betelgeuse and Rigel, to name a few. When a winter storm blocks your view, you can create your own indoor constellations or mix up some starry snacks. Then, challenge a friend to a constellation card game. With winter's short days and Earth offering little food or comfort, many stories of winter constellations share a common theme — hunger and hunting.

SKY MAP FOR THE EVENING HOURS

Turn the map so the direction you are facing is at the bottom.

WHAT TO LOOK FOR IN THE WINTER SKY

Winter boasts more brilliant stars than any other season of the year. Look for star-studded Orion, the Hunter, and he will help you track down and name the constellations of the winter sky.

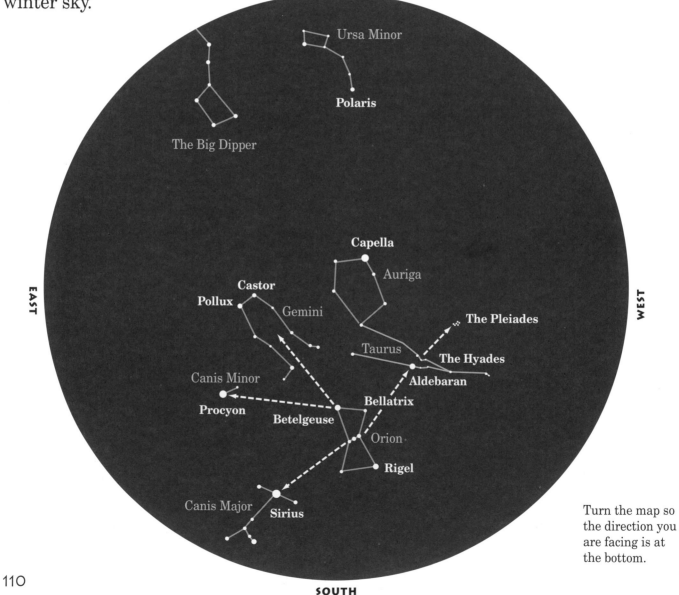

NORTH

Ursa Minor

Polaris

The Big Dipper

EAST

WEST

Capella

Auriga

Castor

Pollux

Gemini

Taurus

The Pleiades

The Hyades

Aldebaran

Canis Minor

Bellatrix

Procyon

Betelgeuse

Orion

Rigel

Canis Major

Sirius

Turn the map so the direction you are facing is at the bottom.

SOUTH

ORION, THE HUNTER

Face south and look up. You'll see three stars close together in a row. These stars make up Orion's belt. Then look for the bright stars at his shoulders (red giant Betelgeuse and hot blue Bellatrix) and his one knee (white Rigel). Hanging from his belt is a three-star sword, one star of which is actually a nebula. On clear nights, look for the three stars that make up Orion's tiny head. Look also for the arcs of stars that form his club and shield (see stories pages 86 and 120).

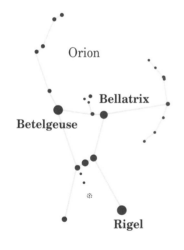

PROCYON

Follow a line east from Orion's shoulders to find Procyon, the main star in the constellation Canis Minor, the Little Dog.

ALDEBARAN

Follow a line from Orion's belt to the northwest and find Aldebaran, the yellow eye of Taurus, the Bull (see story page 119). A V of stars, with Aldebaran at the end of one arm, outlines the bull's face. The V is an open star cluster called the Hyades, best viewed with binoculars.

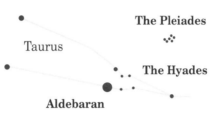

THE PLEIADES

West of Aldebaran is a brilliant star cluster called the Pleiades (see story page 122). Six hot blue stars are easily seen with the naked eye, but you can see more than four hundred with a large telescope.

SIRIUS

Follow a line from Orion's belt to the southeast to the brightest star in the winter sky. Sirius is the collar of Canis Major, the Great Dog (see story page 120).

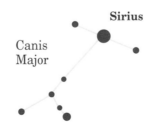

CASTOR AND POLLUX

Northeast of Orion, look for these bright stars that pinpoint the heads of Gemini, the Twins (see stories pages 119 and 136). Their bodies are two lines of stars that arch toward Orion.

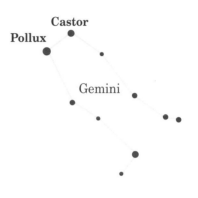

CAPELLA

Close to overhead on a midwinter evening, look for dazzling golden Capella, the main star in Auriga, the Charioteer. Capella sits on the edge of the Milky Way.

111

INDOOR CONSTELLATIONS

When it's too cloudy or stormy outside, make your own indoor constellations so star watching can be an everyday event.

CONSTELLATION CANDLES

Yukon kids decorate these candleholders with their familiar circumpolar star patterns — the Big Dipper, Cassiopeia and Polaris — but you can choose any stars you like. Why not make your own birthday constellation (see page 101)?

You'll need:
a clean, smooth, empty tin can
pliers
a fine-tipped permanent marker
a sharp nail
a hammer
a tealight candle

1.
Use the pliers to flatten any sharp bits around the top edge of the can.

2.
Using the marker, make a dot-to-dot of the stars or constellations of your choice on the can.

3.
Fill the can with water and freeze until solid. Remove from the freezer.

4.
Lay the can on its side on a hard surface, such as a flat rock or cutting board, and have an adult hold it firmly in place.

5.
Hammer the nail into each dot to make small holes in the can.

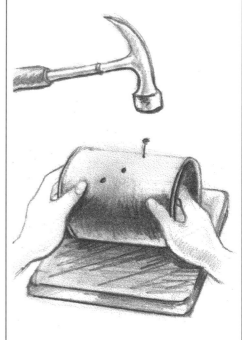

6.
Shake out the ice. Place the candle in the bottom of the can.

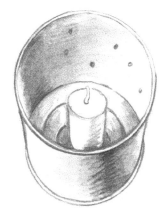

7.
Ask an adult to light the candle. Never leave a burning candle unattended.

CONSTELLATION FLASHCARDS

Test your knowledge of star names with constellation cards.

You'll need:
ten pieces of cardboard the size of playing cards
a flashlight
a pencil

1.
On each piece of cardboard, trace around the flashlight with a pencil.

2.
Using the star maps in this book, copy a constellation in each circle. Poke tiny holes through each star with a sharp pencil.

3.
Label one side of each card with the constellation's name.

4.
In a dark room, place the flashlight on the circle and shine the light through the card onto a wall. Take turns guessing the names of the constellations.

COSMIC MILK AND COOKIES

MOON COOKIES

Prepare this E.T. (Extra Tasty) snack ahead of stargazing time.

You'll need:
175 mL (¾ c.) margarine or butter
250 mL (1 c.) white sugar
1 egg
0.5 L (2 c.) white flour
2 mL (½ tsp.) baking soda
2 mL (½ tsp.) cream of tartar
5 mL (1 tsp.) vanilla
mixing bowls
a wooden spoon
wax paper
a cookie sheet
a kitchen knife
a rolling pin
a spatula
oven mitts

1.
In a large mixing bowl, cream together the margarine, sugar and egg.

2.
In a medium bowl, combine the flour, baking soda and cream of tartar. Stir into the creamed mixture a little at a time.

3.
When the dough is completely mixed, stir in the vanilla.

4.
Place a large piece of wax paper on the counter and scoop the dough onto it.

5.
Roll up the dough in the wax paper so it looks like a long sausage with a diameter of about 5 cm (2 in.). Seal the ends and refrigerate the dough for at least an hour.

6.
With an adult's help, preheat the oven to 180°C (350°F). Grease the cookie sheet with a small amount of margarine.

7.
Remove the wax paper from the dough and use the kitchen knife to cut cookies 1 cm (½ in.) thick. You can also cut dough circles into half-moon or star-shaped cookies. Form a ball with the leftover dough and roll on a board dusted with a little flour. Cut out more shapes.

8.
Using the spatula, place the cookies on the cookie sheet.

9.
Bake each batch for 8 to 10 minutes.

10.
With an adult's help, use oven mitts to remove cookies from the oven. Allow the cookies to cool for a few minutes before transferring them to a plate with the spatula. When they are cool, store them in an airtight container.

STARDUST DRINK MIX

You'll want to keep this drink mix on hand — it's bursting with flavor!

You'll need:
250 mL (1 c.) skim milk powder
250 mL (1 c.) non-dairy creamer
175 mL (¾ c.) sugar
150 mL (⅔ c.) unsweetened cocoa powder
50 mL (¼ c.) decaffeinated instant coffee
113 g (1 package) vanilla instant pudding mix
a large mixing bowl
a wooden spoon
a thermos

1.
Pour all ingredients into a large bowl and mix well with a wooden spoon, a whisk or a fork.

2.
For a hot drink, for each person, mix 45 mL (3 tbsp.) of the mixture with 250 mL (1 c.) of boiling water. Pour into a thermos.

3.
For a cold drink, dissolve 45 mL (3 tbsp.) of the mixture in 45 mL (3 tbsp.) of boiling water in a measuring cup. Add enough cold water to make 250 mL (1 c.). Place ice in the thermos and fill with 250 mL (1 c.) of the drink per person.

4.
Store any unused powder in an airtight container.

HEAVENLY WORD GAMES

Play these games while you're waiting for the stars to come out.

CONSTELLATION CONCENTRATION

You'll need:
scissors
several pieces of light cardboard or thick paper
a pencil
a ruler

1.

Cut the piece of cardboard into twenty squares, 5 cm x 5 cm (2 in. x 2 in.).

2.

On each of two squares, draw identical pictures of a constellation or heavenly object to make a pair. Repeat with different constellations or objects until you have ten pairs.

3.

Turn all the squares face down and mix them around.

4.

Players alternate turning over two squares. If a player finds a pair, that player gets to keep the squares and try again. If the squares do not match, the player turns them face down again, where they were, and another player takes a turn.

5.

Players take turns until all the pairs have been collected. The winner is the one with the most squares.

HEAVENLY CATEGORIES

Have you ever seen an all-star game, driven in a car named after a constellation or eaten a chocolate bar named after a planet? You can see night sky words like these all around you.

Think of the different ways night sky words are used in advertising: for car names, sports teams, snack foods or movie promotions, to name a few. Challenge your friends to see who can come up with the longest list of night sky words used in the categories you select.

STARS OUT

Try this wacky hangman-style game using constellation names.

Draw dots on the top of a piece of paper to represent the Big Dipper. Below that draw dashes to represent each letter in a constellation name. Challenge a friend to guess the letters in your constellation's name. Every time your friend chooses a wrong letter, cross out a star in the Big Dipper. Every time a correct letter is chosen, write it in its correct place(s) over the dashes. Your friend tries to guess the name before running out of stars in the Big Dipper. Then it's your turn to guess a constellation name of your friend's choosing.

♈ ♉ ♊ ♋ ♌ ♍ ♎ ♏ ♐ ♑ ♒ ♓

WINTER ZODIAC STORIES

ARIES, THE RAM

Aries, the Ram, is traditionally considered the first sign of the zodiac. This winter constellation reminded the ancient Greeks of spring, when light and warmth return to the land, lambs are born and sheep are sheared.

Odysseus and his men, sailing home from the Trojan War, landed on an island inhabited by Cyclops — one-eyed giants. A shepherd-Cyclops named Polyphemus captured and imprisoned the sailors in his sealed cave. Each night, Polyphemus returned with his flock and ate two of his prisoners for supper.

Desperate to escape the dark and dangerous cave, Odysseus devised a plan. One day, while Polyphemus was minding his sheep, Odysseus sharpened a piece of tree root into a spear. That night, after Polyphemus's dinner, Odysseus offered him wine. Polyphemus drank several glasses and asked Odysseus for his name. He replied, "No Man." Polyphemus said, "I will eat you last."

When the giant fell asleep, Odysseus and his men plunged the spear into the Cyclops's one eye, blinding him. He woke with a roar that brought his friends running from all over the island. "No Man is trying to kill me!" shrieked Polyphemus. His fellow Cyclops laughed and went home. The next morning, Odysseus and his men hid under the bellies of the sheep and escaped when Polyphemus let his flock out of the cave. It was the ram, or male sheep, that helped Odysseus escape from the cave.

♈ ♉ ♊ ♋ ♌ ♍ ♎ ♏ ♐ ♑ ♒ ♓

GEMINI, THE TWINS

In the constellation Gemini, the Romans saw two boys standing side by side, each holding a spear. They named the two brightest stars — the heads of the twins — Castor and Pollux.

According to the myth, Castor was a human and Pollux was a god. As children they were inseparable, training first as athletes and later as fierce warriors. When Castor was killed in battle, Pollux begged Zeus to reunite them. Zeus allowed Pollux to split his time — half with the other gods of Olympus and half with Castor in Hades. This arrangement is shown in the sky with the rising and setting of Castor and Pollux. When Castor appears in the east, Pollux is right behind him. When Castor sets in the west, Pollux follows him.

TAURUS, THE BULL

When Zeus saw the beautiful Europa, daughter of King Agenor of Tyre, he wanted to catch her attention. He transformed himself into a pure white bull and followed Europa into a field of flowers beside the sea.

At first Europa was startled by the beast, but when she looked into his gentle, big eyes, she lost all fear. She made a wreath of flowers, hung it around the bull's neck and patted his head. Then she asked if she could ride on his back, and the bull knelt down so she could climb up. She rode up and down the beach, laughing and waving to her friends.

Suddenly, without warning, the bull turned and galloped toward the sea. Europa clung to his horns in terror, but found that she was not getting wet — the bull was flying above the waves. When they landed in Crete, the bull became Zeus again, declared his love and crowned Europa's head with royal jewels.

THE STORY OF OSIRIS AND ISIS: A MURDER THRILLER

Osiris, the god of light, was Egypt's first king. Since then the Egyptian people have connected him with the constellation Orion, the Hunter. His devoted Queen Isis has remained famous as Sirius, the Dog Star, the brightest star in the sky.

Together Osiris and his wife Isis ruled Egypt. After years of war and chaos, Osiris brought peace to the land. He was kind, clever and extremely popular. When Osiris traveled abroad, Isis stayed behind and ruled in his place. She kept a sharp eye on his jealous brother, Set, the god of darkness. Osiris trusted Set, but Isis knew he was evil.

One night when Isis was away, Osiris invited his brother and other important men for dinner. Set arrived with an exquisite box carved from Lebanese cedar, covered in jewels and gilded with gold. Set boasted that when the meal was done, whoever fit in the box could have it. The feasting went on for hours, and the box was a source of great curiosity and discussion. Various guests climbed inside, but found it too big or too small. Finally Osiris decreed that it was meant for him. The unsuspecting king got in and shouted that it was the perfect size. Peering down at him, Set laughed, slammed the lid shut and locked it. Loyal guests tried to release Osiris, but Set had his wicked henchmen carry off the box and throw it in the Nile River. When the news reached Isis, Set had already crowned himself king.

With no time for tears and her life in danger, Isis immediately began the long search for Osiris's body. She hoped her powers as a goddess could restore his life. Failing that, her husband needed a proper burial or his spirit would remain in limbo forever. Trudging from village to village along the banks of the Nile, Isis could feel their baby — the rightful heir to the Egyptian throne — moving inside her.

With the help of faithful subjects, Isis finally found the coffin. Inside, Osiris looked asleep but neither her kiss nor her magic could revive him. Grief and exhaustion were soon swept aside as her son, Horus, was born. But in Isis's distraction, the coffin was left unguarded. Set found it, cut Osiris into fourteen pieces and scattered him in the river. Isis managed to find thirteen parts and carved the fourteenth from a piece of pine. When Osiris was wrapped in linen and properly prepared for the afterlife, he rose to the sky as the constellation Orion, where he remains to this day.

The next time you look at Orion, find the three stars on his belt and then look southeast to Isis as Sirius. Can you see Osiris looking tenderly over his shoulder as they sail across the night sky?

THE SEVEN HUNGRY DANCERS: A MYSTERY

The blue-white stars of the Pleiades star cluster are so bright they seem to dance on cold nights. The cluster appears on the eastern horizon at sunset in November and, as winter deepens, rises higher and higher, evening by evening. The Onondagas of New York State tell this story, which follows the cluster as it rises and dances in the winter sky.

A hunting party found a beautiful lake, its water teeming with fish, its banks covered with berries and the surrounding forest filled with deer. The hunters brought their families to the lake so they could live through the winter on its plentiful harvest.

By autumn, when the longhouses were built, there was little to do. Seven young hunters went to the forest to dance the time away. Day after day, they left for the forest and danced. One day, an old man with white hair and a robe covered in white feathers visited their dancing grounds. He warned the boys to stop dancing or evil would come. The boys ignored his warning and kept dancing. The old man returned many times, but the boys danced on.

One day, the smallest boy, who was getting hungry from all the dancing, suggested they bring food to the dancing grounds. However, when the boys asked if they could eat their meals in the forest, their parents said they must eat at home.

The boys decided to dance without eating. They danced on and on until their heads grew light with hunger. They danced until they started to rise off the ground, little by little. One boy noticed they were rising into the air and called to the others, "Don't look down. Something bad might happen."

A woman saw the boys and called for them to come down. But they wouldn't even look down — they just kept dancing and rising higher in the air. She ran for help. The boys' parents came running with food and pleaded with their sons to come back and eat.

Only the smallest boy looked down, and he fell to the ground as a shooting star. The other six boys kept dancing and rising until they turned into stars. They have remained in the sky, dancing, ever since.

REGULAR GUEST APPEARANCES:
THE PLANETS

Move over Sun, Moon and stars! In this section, it's the planets that shine. Get ready to have your planetary questions answered: Do planets move on a straight path? Make a planet plotter and find out. Meteoroid, meteor, meteorite — what's the difference? Morphing meteors will clue you in. What's the story behind the planets' names? Romans will shed light on that. How can a turnip ruin your life? Feather Woman learned the hard way. And find out how the Hero Twins followed the orbit of Venus before turning into the Sun and the Moon.

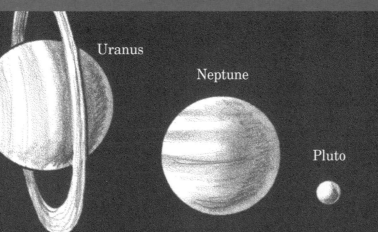

Saturn

Uranus

Neptune

Pluto

PLANET WATCH

Planets don't twinkle like stars do, so this makes them easy to spot. But they do vary in brightness, so it can be tricky to identify which planet is which. All planets travel near the ecliptic, but the only ones you can see without binoculars or a telescope are Mercury, Venus, Mars, Jupiter and Saturn. With the help of space probes and high-powered telescopes, astronomers keep finding more amazing details about our planet neighbors. They're even discovering new moons!

MERCURY

Tiny Mercury is the hardest planet to spot and can be seen for only a few weeks a year. It changes its position from one night to the next, but it's always low in the sky. Mercury is best seen just after sunset in the spring or before sunrise in the autumn.

If you do spot Mercury, you're seeing a dead, hot, small and airless planet.

VENUS

Venus is the most dazzling planet seen from Earth. An atmosphere of thick clouds around this planet reflects sunlight, making it appear ten times brighter than the brightest nighttime star.

Venus never appears high overhead — only near the rising or setting Sun, as does Mercury. For about six months, it is the "morning star" in the east before disappearing behind the rising Sun. For several months, Venus cannot be seen at all. Then it reappears as the "evening star" in the west. After six months, it disappears into the sunset only to reappear as the morning star a few weeks later.

Venus is a hot planet with an atmosphere of deadly carbon dioxide. Life as we know it is impossible on Venus.

MARS

Mars appears reddish orange in color. Compared to other planets, Mars moves quickly through the background stars making it fun to track. You can't see it move in one night, but you'll notice it changing place over days and weeks. Every two years, Mars appears to retrace its steps — moving westward compared to the other stars and then eastward with the other stars. This happens when Mars is closest to Earth and faster moving Earth overtakes and passes slower moving Mars.

The surface of Mars looks like a wasteland — covered with extinct volcanoes, red dusty deserts, craters and canyons. It has polar ice caps just like Earth, but its overall average surface temperature is –50˚C (–58˚ F).

HEAVENLY NAMES

The Romans named the planets after their gods — Mercury the messenger god, Mars the god of war and so on. Three planets were discovered after Roman times but were given Roman names, too: Uranus after Saturn's father, Neptune for the god of the sea and Pluto, the god of the dead.

Q: Did you have fun at the party on Mercury?

A: No, there was no atmosphere.

MORE PLANETS TO WATCH

JUPITER

Second to Venus in brightness, Jupiter is more than three hundred times bigger and eleven times wider than Earth. Jupiter travels at a slow speed, moving westward across the sky. Viewed from Earth, it seems to spend a year in each constellation of the zodiac and then, after twelve years, it starts its journey across the sky again.

Thirty moons orbit Jupiter. The four big ones — Io, Europa, Ganymede and Callisto — are about the size of Earth's Moon and can be seen through a small telescope.

When you look at bright, gigantic Jupiter, it's hard to imagine it's really a huge ball of swirling, freezing gas.

SATURN

Saturn is the second-largest, slowest moving and most distant of all the visible planets. This gas giant is a yellowish color, so it looks like a bright star, which makes it hard to identify as a planet.

When you spot Saturn, you won't see that it has about twenty-eight moons. But a beautiful set of rings made of ice crystals surrounding the planet can be seen through a small telescope.

Q: What did Mars say to Saturn?

A: Give me a ring sometime.

HOW BRIGHT ARE THE PLANETS?

A planet's brightness is measured the same way as a star's brightness (see page 42).

Venus is the brightest object in the night sky, other than the Moon, at about –4.

Jupiter is hot on Venus's heels at –3.

Mars's brightness varies from –3 to 2.

Saturn shines in at about 0.

Rarely seen Mercury can be as bright as –3

Neptune, Uranus and Pluto are not visible to the naked eye.

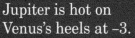
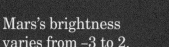

MAKE A PLANET PLOTTER

In ancient times, people called planets wandering stars. They noticed that the Sun, Moon and stars slide smoothly across the sky. But the planets change in brightness, seem to speed up and slow down, and sometimes even go backward.

Do planets really wander? You can see for yourself if you make a planet plotter and trace a planet's path over several weeks.

You'll need:
a square box, about 30 cm (12 in.) in length, height and width
a square of rigid, clear plastic, 15 cm x 15 cm (6 in. x 6 in.), such as the window from a see-through package
scissors
permanent markers
tape
string
small colored stickers, numbered 1 to 7

1.

Cut holes slightly smaller than the square of plastic at opposite ends of the box.

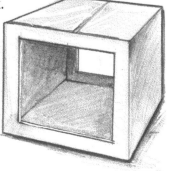

2.

Cut a hole in the side of the box big enough to fit your hand.

3.

With a marker, draw two lines on the plastic sheet at a right angle to each other. Tape the plastic inside the box over one of the end holes.

4.

Cut two lengths of string longer than the sheet of plastic.

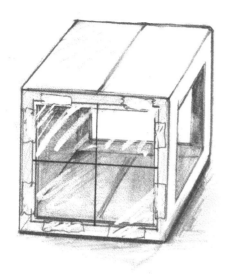

5.

Tape the pieces of string at a right angle across the hole at the other end of the box.

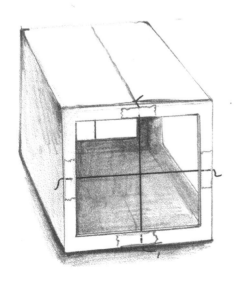

USING THE PLANET PLOTTER

1.

Look along the ecliptic for a planet in the evening sky (see page 126). Locate at least three nearby bright stars.

2.

With a marker in one hand, hold the string end of the planet plotter up to your eye and look through the box at the planet. Line up the point where the strings meet with the point where the marker lines meet, keeping the planet in the center.

3.

Holding the box steady, put your marker hand through the side hole. Put dots on the plastic sheet to mark the location of the three nearby stars.

4.

With the sights lined up to each other and the three nearby stars lined up with their dots, place sticker 1 at the planet's location.

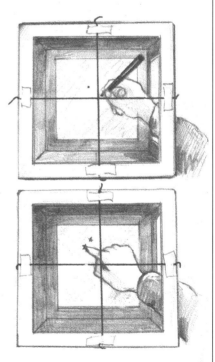

5.

For the next six nights, look through the plotter at the planet and repeat step 4 using the numbered stickers in order.

6.

After a week, review the planet's path. Did it wander?

IDENTIFIABLE FLYING OBJECTS

It's not a star and it's not a planet, so what is it? Many other objects, big and small, travel through space. Add these to your list of what to watch for in the night sky.

COMETS

- Comets look like blurry streaks in the night sky. Made of ice, gas, dust and rocks, they can be up to 20 km (12 mi.) across. When they travel near the Sun, comets are blasted by radiation and start to fall apart. Then, tails of rock and ice as long as 100 million km (62 million mi.) stream out behind them.

- Comets travel around the Sun like planets do, but they journey far into the outer solar system. However, astronomers have identified enough comets to be able to predict when one is due in the inner solar system. Check your local paper or radio for best viewing times.

- Millions of comets orbit the Sun.

ASTEROIDS

- The word asteroid means "starlike body."

- Known as minor planets, asteroids range in size from as small as a house to as big as a large state or province.

- With binoculars, zoom in on the Moon's craters. You're probably looking at the results of asteroid crash landings.

- Most asteroids are found in the asteroid belt between Mars and Jupiter.

- The asteroid Vesta can sometimes be seen with the naked eye. You can see dozens more with a telescope.

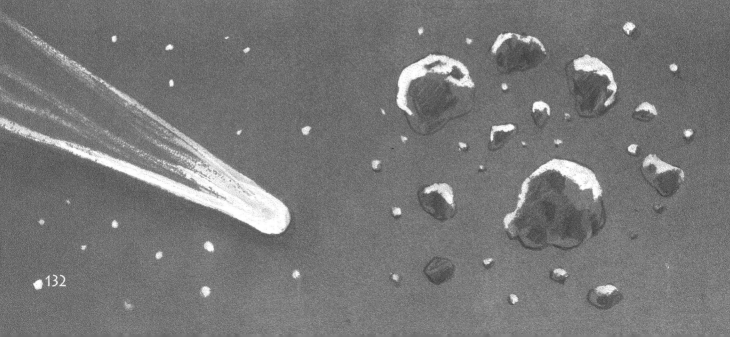

MORPHING METEORITES

- Meteoroids are formed during cosmic collisions and were once part of an asteroid, comet, planet or moon. Most are as light and small as a grain of sand, but a few are as big and heavy as an empty airplane.

- A meteoroid is a small chunk of rock in space. When it enters Earth's atmosphere, catches fire and burns up, it's called a meteor or shooting star. It's not a star at all, but the term describes what seems to be happening in the sky. A meteorite is what's left of a meteoroid when it hits Earth.

- Although thousands of meteorites hit Earth every day, most are too small for you to find or identify.

LAUNCHED FROM EARTH

- Some objects in the night sky take off from Earth.

- Planes move quickly across the sky and have a red light on the left wing, green light on the right, white flashing lights on both wings and red light on the plane's belly.

- Satellites have no blinking lights, but their brightness can change as sunlight reflects off their surfaces. They may take several minutes to cross the sky and can be confused with bright stars.

- The International Space Station looks like a very bright satellite. When a space shuttle is docked with it, the space station appears even brighter.

133

MORNING STAR AND FEATHER WOMAN: A ROMANCE

Dazzling white Venus has inspired love stories around the world. Blackfoot elders from the plains of Canada and the United States told the love story of Morning Star and Feather Woman. In their story, Venus is Morning Star, the Spider Man's lodge is Corona Borealis, the Northern Crown, and the giant turnip is the North Star.

One spring night, Feather Woman slept out on the prairie grass. At dawn she looked up at the sky and whispered, "I wish I could marry Morning Star."

Some time later, Feather Woman was walking alone when a stranger appeared on the trail in front of her. He held a juniper branch covered in cobwebs. Frightened, Feather Woman turned to run, but the stranger called, "Don't be afraid. I am Morning Star. I have loved you from afar, and once you said you loved me, too. Come with me and be my wife." Feather Woman looked at him, and her heart filled with love. She agreed to go with Morning Star without even saying good-bye to her family.

Morning Star placed a strand of cobweb on the ground. He told Feather Woman to shut her eyes and step on it. When Feather Woman opened her eyes again, she was standing in the land of the Star People. Morning Star said, "Walk carefully. We are near the lodge of the Spider Man. The Star People use his webs to climb up and down between Earth and the sky."

Morning Star took Feather Woman to the tipi of his parents, Sun and Moon. Moon, his mother, greeted Feather Woman warmly, but Sun told her to obey the laws of the Star Country if she wished to be happy.

In weeks to come, Moon taught Feather Woman how to tan hides white and dig for roots to eat. Moon gave her a special digging stick. Once, when Feather Woman found an enormous turnip near the Spider Man's lodge, Moon told her it was sacred and must never be dug up.

In time, Morning Star and Feather Woman had a son they named Star Boy. Feather Woman's happiness was complete — but the forbidden turnip fascinated her. What could be under it that was so important?

One day when Feather Woman was alone, she decided to dig up the turnip. But it was too big. Two cranes came to her aid and worked at

the ground with their sharp bills. Together they finally uprooted the turnip, and Feather Woman looked down the hole. Below, she saw Earth and her own people. She felt homesick.

Late in the day, Feather Woman rolled the turnip back into its hole and slowly returned to her husband. Sun sensed she had disobeyed and said she must return to Earth. Moon and Morning Star begged him to forgive Feather Woman, but Sun said she would never be happy again with the Star People and must leave.

Sadly, Morning Star wrapped Star Boy and Feather Woman in white buckskin. He took them to the Spider Man's lodge and gently let them down to Earth with spiderwebs.

Feather Woman's people accepted her back, but she grew pale and thin. Each night she sat on a ridge and watched for Morning Star to rise in the sky. At dawn one morning, she called out for forgiveness, but Morning Star called back, "Too late, too late," and traveled on. Soon after, Feather Woman died of a broken heart.

THE HERO TWINS:
AN ACTION THRILLER

In Guatemala, the Maya told a story about two young gods — the Hero Twins — who set out to defeat the lords of the underworld and make Earth ready for human beings. In this story, the twins' ball court is in the constellation Gemini, the Twins, and the path to Xibalba, the underworld, is the dark slash in the Milky Way near Cygnus, the Swan. The twins have magical powers and can change shape, disappear into fire and re-emerge whole — all powers the Maya saw in the orbit of Venus.

The Hero Twins were expert players of tlachtli, a game like soccer. Deep in Xibalba, the lords heard the thumping of the twins practicing on their ball court above and challenged the twins to a match. The twins accepted and journeyed down the black path to the underworld. But the twins were careful — they knew they would die if the lords outsmarted them in a match of wits or defeated them in a match of tlachtli in Xibalba.

The twins didn't know the names of the lords or what to expect, so they sent ahead a mosquito to bite the lords. The first two lords did not react when bitten by the mosquito, so the twins realized they were only wooden puppets. The twelve real lords cried out, blaming one another for the painful stings. The twins listened and memorized their names. Then, when they entered the throne room, the twins passed right by the puppets and greeted the lords by name.

The lords realized the twins were clever opponents and decided to outsmart them before the first game of the match. They invited the twins to sit on two thrones, but the twins saw that the seats were red-hot and declined. When their trick didn't fool the twins, the lords took them to a House of Darkness and gave them cigars and pine sticks, challenging the twins to burn them all night but return them whole in the morning. The twins put macaw feathers on the ends of the sticks and fireflies on the tips of the cigars so they looked as if they were on fire. In the morning, the lords were stunned to see the cigars and sticks still whole.

It was time for the first game of tlachtli, and the lords won in a close contest. By evening, the score stood at Lords of Xibalba 1, Hero Twins 0.

The lords demanded the twins deliver four baskets of flowers by the next morning and then locked them in a House of Knives. The twins avoided the slashing knives, but found no

Story continued next page

flowers in their prison. They called on the army ants for help. The ants filed out under the locked door and into the lords' garden.There they cut and carried back enough flowers to fill the baskets. The lords were amazed when the twins produced the required flowers in the morning.

In the second day's game of tlachtli, the twins and the lords tied. The score remained unchanged at Lords of Xibalba 1, Hero Twins 0.

Angry at not winning the match outright, the lords threw the twins into a House of Cold for the night. The twins survived by building a huge bonfire. Then the lords threw them into a House of Jaguars, but the twins outsmarted the lords by tossing the jaguars bones to chew.

Finally, in a House of Bats, the twins avoided being bitten by changing shape and hiding inside their blowguns. But when one twin peeked out to see if dawn was near, a vampire bat bit off his head and dropped it onto the ball court. The lords were sure they would win the match now. But there was still some night left, and the other twin called all the animals for help. The coati, one of the animals, arrived with a squash, and the twin carved a false head out of it to place on his brother's neck. When the twins stepped onto the court in the morning, they swapped the false head for the real one and defeated the lords.

The score was tied at Lords of Xibalba 1, Hero Twins 1.

After the game, the lords heated an oven to cook a special drink. The twins surprised the lords by joining hands and diving into the flames. When the fire consumed the twins, the lords declared they had finally won. They threw the twins' ashes into the river.

But downstream and several days later, the twins walked out of the water whole. They disguised themselves as beggars and performed dances, songs and magic tricks for the lords. They seemed to set fire to houses but the houses were unharmed. They made a dog disappear, then reappear and wag its tail. One beggar even seemed to kill the other but then to bring him back to life. The lords of Xibalba were so impressed, their two leaders asked the beggars to kill them and bring them back to life, too. The beggars agreed to kill the lords but, once they were dead, refused to bring them back to life. When the beggars revealed themselves as the Hero Twins, the remaining lords ran to hide in deep ravines and crevices.

The twins decided no lord of the underworld would ever again be able to play tlachtli or hold powers on Earth. The creator god, the Heart of Heaven, saw that Earth was now safe for people. He placed the Hero Twins in the sky as the Sun and the Moon. Then he made human beings out of cornmeal. The humans looked up on the first dawn and saw the Moon, the planet Venus and then the rising Sun. They thanked the Heart of Heaven for their creation and for the beauty of Earth and sky.

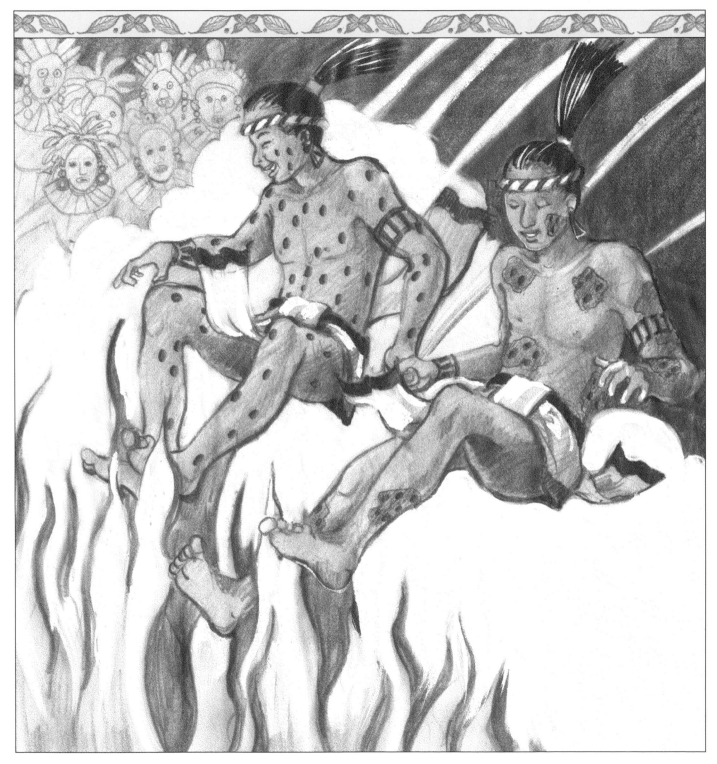

GLOSSARY

asteroid: a small object made of rock and up to 1000 km (about 620 mi.) in diameter

astrology: an ancient, non-scientific belief that the positions of the Sun, Moon and planets among the stars influence people's lives

astronomy: the scientific study of the universe beyond Earth's atmosphere

celestial equator: an imaginary line across the sky directly above Earth's equator

celestial pole: an imaginary point in the sky directly above the North or South Pole. Polaris, the North Star, lies almost exactly on the north celestial pole. All stars seem to revolve around the poles.

circumpolar stars: stars that do not set below the horizon at any time during the year for a particular location on Earth. In the Northern Hemisphere, the stars closest to Polaris, the North Star, which is near the celestial pole, are circumpolar.

comet: a small object made of rock and ice that follows a long orbit around the Sun. As it approaches and is heated by the Sun, a comet may release gas and dust in a glowing tail that streams away from the Sun.

constellation: an area of the sky named after an animal, person, monster or non-living object. The name is usually based on the outline or shape the stars appear to make. Astronomers have divided the sky into eighty-eight constellations.

ecliptic: the path the Sun seems to take across the sky. The planets also appear close to this path.

eclipse: an event during which all or part of the light from one space body is cut off by another.

equator: an imaginary line circling Earth, east to west, equally distant from the North and South Poles

equinox: the name given to two dates around March 21 and September 21 each year, when the Sun, traveling on the ecliptic, crosses the celestial equator. See also **solstice**.

galaxy: an immense group of stars, dust and gas held together by gravity and separated from other galaxies by vast areas of space

gravity: a force of attraction possessed by anything that is made of matter

meteor: a lump of space rock falling toward Earth from space. Traveling at speeds up to 100 000 km/h (62 100 mph), the rock heats up in Earth's atmosphere and emits light for a few seconds before burning up.

meteorite: a chunk of rock that has reached Earth's surface from space

meteoroid: a small chunk of rock, often the remnant of a comet or asteroid, traveling in space

Milky Way: our home galaxy, made up of our Sun, the solar system and more than 400 billion stars

moon: a natural satellite of a planet. Our Moon is the natural satellite of Earth.

nebula: a huge cloud of interstellar gas and dust, sometimes dark and sometimes glowing from the light of stars nearby or inside the cloud

orbit: the curved path taken by one sky object moving around another

planet: an object more than 1000 km (about 620 mi.) in diameter that orbits a star and is seen by reflected starlight

red giant: a very large, aging star that has a low surface temperature and is reddish in color

satellite: a natural or artificial space object that orbits a planet

solstice: the name given to two dates every year around June 21 and December 21, when the Sun, traveling along the ecliptic, reaches the farthest point north or south of the celestial equator that it can travel in the sky. See also **equinox**.

star: a very hot space body, made mostly of hydrogen and helium gas, that produces and emits its own light

star cluster: a group of stars traveling through space that are held together by gravity, such as the Pleiades

white dwarf: a dying star that has collapsed down to an object about the size of Earth and has a temperature of about 10 000°C (18 000°F)

zodiac: a band of constellations centered on the ecliptic through which the Sun, Moon and planets appear to move during the year

Q: What does Perseus do when he gets dirty?

A: He takes a meteor shower.

INDEX

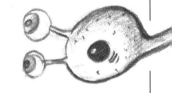

**The Sun Is a Star,
Page 10, Answers**

1. False;
2. False;
3. False;
4. False;
5. False;
6. False